The Blessing

Wayde I. Goodall

with

Rosalyn Goodall

D1380190

THE BLESSING by Wayde I. Goodall with Rosalyn Goodall
Published by Creation House
A Strang Company
600 Rinehart Road
Lake Mary, Florida 32746
www.creationhouse.com

Unless otherwise noted, all Scripture quotations are from the
Holy Bible, New International Version. Copyright © 1973,
1978, 1984, International Bible Society. Used by permission.

Scripture quotations marked KJV are from the King James
Version of the Bible.

Cover design by Terry Clifton

Library of Congress Control Number: 2004117098
International Standard Book Number: 1-59185-732-5

05 06 07 08 09— 987654321
Printed in the United States of America

ACKNOWLEDGMENTS

It is an honor to write with the editorial team at Creation House. There is no question that Creation House and the numerous publications that Stephen Strang has produced are touching the kingdom of God in incredible ways. Their constant focus on what God is doing through the charismatic movement and pertinent Christian issues is a blessing to the church—worldwide.

I also want to express deep appreciation for the assistance of Dr. Thomas E. Trask, chairman of the Pentecostal World Fellowship, cochairman of the Pentecostal/Charismatic Churches of North America, and general superintendent of the Assemblies of God. The first edition of *The Blessing*, which was published by Zondervan, is no longer in print. Dr. Trask and I coauthored the first printing and now he has kindly permitted me to do a revision of that work under my name. His contributions to the Pentecostal/Charismatic Church are among the highest in the twenty-first century.

Thirdly, I want to thank my wife, Rosalyn. She is not only a wonderful wife and mother, she is really the coauthor of everything I write. Rosalyn is an instructor in technical and professional writing, and her hours of editing, her proofreading skills, and her dedication to excellence are tremendous gifts to me. In fact, she is the greatest gift I have on this earth. Thanks, Roz, for all you do.

CONTENTS

PREFACE

THE DECADENCE AND darkness of our nation is more profound than it has been since the founding of this nation more than two centuries ago. The only power that can cleanse and restore this nation is the power of Christ."[1]

The twentieth and twenty-first centuries have experienced the greatest technological growth of any century since the beginning of mankind, but also saw more people become followers of Christ than at any other time in church history. In his article entitled "Nine Global Trends in Religion," Ron Sellers explains that "many thinkers have predicted the demise of religion as human understanding and technology advances. Yet neither state-sponsored atheism nor sciences have proven to be religion's undoing. In advanced technological nations such as the United States and under the persecution of Communist leaders in China and Cuba, religion continues to thrive."[2] On one hand, we have more evil, destruction, humanism, and mistrust of leadership; on the other hand, the church of Jesus Christ is growing in unprecedented ways throughout the world.

Not only are tens of thousands of people coming to Christ every day throughout the world, but another New Testament phenomena has become the experience of millions of Christians. That is, the baptism in the Holy Spirit as recorded in Acts 2:4. This Spirit baptism is no longer just an experience that

1

happens to those who are part of a Pentecostal church; it has occurred in Christians' lives in most denominational groups that we know of. Michael Green, an advisor to the archbishop of Canterbury, and author and lecturer R. Paul Stevens wrote this about major forces impacting Christianity during the twentieth century:

> The worldwide movement of the Holy Spirit, which began to make itself felt in the year 1900, first with the Pentecostal movement, but by the middle of the century in the neo-Pentecostal or charismatic surge which has swept through almost all denominations and is unquestionably the most influential Christian emphasis in our times.... This movement lays great stress on the sovereign power of the Spirit to break into the lives of individuals and churches with supernatural grace and manifestations, which the old rationalism had almost persuaded the churches was a thing of the past.[3]

God is pouring out his Spirit on Christians throughout the world. Hundreds of years before Christ, the prophet Joel said, "In the last days, God says, I will pour out my Spirit on all people" (Acts 2:17). Peter referred to Joel's statement to explain to unbelievers what was happening when they observed more than a hundred people who had received the baptism in the Holy Spirit. Peter continued, "The promise is for you and your children and for all who are far off—for all whom the Lord our God will call" (Acts 2:39). We believe that outside of the born-again experience of people making Jesus Christ the Lord of their lives, the next greatest experience a Christian can receive is the baptism in the Holy Spirit.

In this book I desire to speak to three basic groups of people. First, I want to speak to the many who have received this experience and might not know exactly what has happened to them. As you will see, the Bible is full of teachings and theological insight about this experience and manifestations that seem to accompany those who have received the Holy Spirit baptism. Multitudes of hungry Protestants and Catholics throughout the world have had this experience, but might not completely understand the biblical reasons why they received this blessing or what they are to do with it.

Second, many people are inquisitive about the baptism in the Holy Spirit. They simply do not know what to believe, but might have observed someone receiving the experience or perhaps have read about it in the Bible or another Christian book. They want to know more. They are hungry for God and whatever His will is for their lives. We hope this book answers many of their questions. Hopefully, when they have more understanding, they will pray for and will receive the experience themselves.

Third are those who have grown up in a Pentecostal denomination. If they have received this experience, I want to remind them of its importance in their lives and how critical it is to be sensitive to the Holy Spirit and His gifts. We can become apathetic and complacent about the things of God, even when we have had wonderful personal experiences. The baptism in the Holy Spirit is meant to give us power that is supernatural so that we may be greater witnesses for Christ. Many have simply held on to this experience and have not let God use them to affect others for Him. As with a stream that stops flowing, the water will become stagnant; so it is with Christians who have received the Spirit baptism. They can become stagnant in their witness. Many say, "Yes, I once received the experience," but because they did not endeavor to be the witness God wanted them to be, they show little fruit of the dynamic Christian life.

It is not my desire to be divisive in the body of Christ. I understand that some segments of the church differ with some of the opinions found in this book. Yet, in view of the overwhelming biblical teaching on the subject and the obvious evidence of worldwide interest, I believe that the teaching I write about is pertinent and timely.

I sincerely pray that this book will make you hungrier for God and all that He has for you. I also pray that you will experience the blessing of the Holy Spirit, and become a greater witness in an increasingly needy world.

Chapter 1

THE OUTPOURING: THE REDISCOVERY OF AZUSA AND ITS SIGNIFICANCE

DIANE'S STRUGGLE WITH deep depression had caused her to be bedridden for three years. Her lifelong battle with emotional pain had finally worn her down to a point where she did not want to talk to people or even leave the darkness of her bedroom to face another day. She knew that if she did not get help, she would die. Counselor after counselor had tried to provide answers for her deep sadness. Desperate, Diane traveled several hundred miles from her home to try one last professional.

During counseling, the Christian psychologist asked Diane if she could remember when her depression had begun. She knew that her sadness had lasted almost forty-eight years. She was now fifty-one. They explored possible events that could have occurred when she was between two and three years of age.

The counselor said, "Diane, do you remember or has anyone told you of any traumatic events that happened to you when you were two or three?"

Diane responded, "I do recall looking at all of my childhood pictures and noticing how alive and happy I was as a baby." She paused for a few seconds then added, "My pictures look like I was enjoying a loving and joyful life until I turned three."

The doctor asked, "Do you appear sad or depressed in your pictures from that point on?"

Diane answered, "As a matter of fact, I do."

This new information gave the psychologist some possible clues to Diane's lifelong struggle. He decided to research that period of her life, and after several sessions, family documentation, and a great deal of hard work, he determined that several boys in Diane's neighborhood had sexually molested her. This terrifying experience had begun Diane's downward spiral of depression. As the years passed, she had gone deeper and deeper into despair.

Gaining this understanding helped Diane tremendously. She began to feel hopeful for the first time in years, and her depression began to lift.

In one counseling session, the doctor asked Diane to try to understand that Jesus had always cared for her. Even in her pain, Jesus had been available to help her. Diane knew this deep down because she had become a Christian when she was a child. She had attended church all of her life and had hoped that God knew of her pain, but she had never understood that He would, or even could, take away her despair. The ministers of her church taught that miracles had ended with the death of the early apostles and that healings and other gifts the early church had experienced were only for them. She had learned that she could read about miracles in the Bible and be encouraged, but not that she could experience them for herself.

The counselor gave Diane an assignment. He said, "Diane, I know you have been unable to stay out of bed for a full day. Spending eighteen hours a day in bed adds to your depression. I will help you gradually work up to a normal amount of bed rest."[1]

One evening, to fill the time that she needed to stay out of bed, Diane decided to attend a local church that was having something called a "revival." The church had been having special services almost every night for several weeks. The crowds of people wanted the services to continue, and there was an unusual presence of the Lord in each service. Diane felt this presence when she first sat down in the pew. At the end of the preacher's message, he asked for people to come to the front of the church if they needed anything from God. Diane thought, *I am going to do this and see what happens.* She responded, knowing that she needed a complete healing.

At the front, Diane met dozens of other people who also had come forward. Some wanted to know Jesus personally. Some wanted an experience called the "baptism in the Holy Spirit." Others, like her, wanted healing for physical or emotional needs. They *all* wanted a deeper experience of God's presence and power.

When the speaker got to Diane, he said, "Lift your hands into the air and surrender your life entirely to Jesus." Diane immediately lifted her hands in the air as an act of surrender to the Lord. Her heart was hungry, and she mentally begged God to hear her cry. The speaker reached out to pray for her, and suddenly Diane felt that the Lord had heard her heart's cry and the prayer of the minister. Diane felt a deep sense of peace, contentment, and the presence of God like never before. She knew that God had touched her emotional pain.

Diane's healing took place almost ten years ago. Since early childhood and until that time, she had never known a year, a month, or even a week without depression and emotional torment. Diane had experienced a miracle from God. Human beings had not been able to heal her; they could not know the depth of her pain nor meet her need. But a merciful God knew her dilemma and healed her completely.

No one can tell Diane that God's miraculous power is not available today as it was in the early church. Diane felt God's touch personally and will never be the same. She has never been so happy and is now running a successful business in Michigan. She frequently weeps as she thinks of the amazing God she is growing to understand.

Diane's story is not unusual. We hear similar stories almost every day. In this book we will describe how people throughout the world are experiencing the blessings of the Holy Spirit and the power of Pentecost today. We have seen people healed physically and emotionally, marriages restored, young people delivered from drugs and addictions, and much more. The same spiritual power that was present in the lives of the New Testament disciples is available to us today. Worldwide, the gifts of the Holy Spirit are being utilized and understood more today than at any time since the first century. More people are becoming Christians and experiencing the power of the Holy Spirit than ever before. And more people, like Diane, are having their needs met through miraculous encounters than at any other time in the history of the church.

The Spark Ignites

The twentieth century could very well be the most significant period of church history since the first-century church. Incredible church growth has occurred throughout the world, and tragically, the blood of Christian martyrs has marked this time as well. Denominations, church fellowships, and Christian organizations passionately endeavoring to spread the message of Jesus Christ have been born by the thousands. Like sparks that begin a forest fire in different locations, sparks of revival lit the world a hundred years ago.

One of those sparks ignited just before the turn of the century in Topeka, Kansas. A man named Charles Fox Parham yearned for a greater ability to be used of God. He was a lay preacher with the Methodist Episcopal Church, and believed that the gifts of the Holy Spirit could be active in his day. In 1898 he began a ministry called The Bethel Healing Home in Topeka. Those who were sick could gather together with Parham and others for prayer. After leasing a home called "Stone's Folly"[2] in Topeka, he began to organize frequent prayer meetings with several people who wanted to seek God. He created a small Bible school,[3] studied the Scriptures concerning spiritual gifts, and prayed that if these gifts were available, God would give them to him and the others in the group. Parham declared that the sole purpose of this small Bible school was "utter abandonment in obedience to the commandments of Jesus, however unconventional and impractical this might seem."[4]

Like many people today, this group of devoted Bible students hungered for more of God. As they studied Scripture, they understood that what God could do in the early church He could do now. Vinson Synan writes in his book *The Holiness Pentecostal Movement in the United States:*

> By December 1900, Parham had led his students through a study of the major tenets of the holiness movement, including sanctification and divine healing. When they arrived at the second chapter of Acts they studied the events that transpired on the day of Pentecost in Jerusalem, including speaking with other tongues. At that juncture, Parham had to leave the school for three days for a speaking engagement. Before leaving, he asked the students to study their Bibles in an effort to find the scriptural evidence for the reception of the baptism with the Holy Spirit. Upon returning he asked the students to state the conclusion of their study, and to his "astonishment" they all answered unanimously that the evidence was "speaking with other tongues." This they deduced from the four recorded occasions[5] in the Book of Acts when tongues accompanied the baptism with the Holy Spirit.[6]

In the following days, Parham and his students decided to pray that they would experience the baptism with the Holy Spirit. On New Year's Eve, the students met for a prayer meeting. Synan writes:

Apparently convinced that his conclusion was a proper interpretation of the Scriptures, Parham and his students conducted a watchnight service on December 31, 1900, which was to continue into the new year. In this service, a student named Agnes N. Ozman requested Parham to lay hands on her head and pray for her to be baptized with the Holy Ghost with the evidence of speaking in tongues. It was after midnight and the first day of the twentieth century when Miss Ozman began "speaking in the Chinese language."[7]

Agnes Ozman had never spoken in this language, yet for three days she spoke it and could not speak in English. Suddenly the experience of the apostles on the Day of Pentecost became something with which this group could identify. When they were together, they "were filled with the Holy Spirit and began to speak in other tongues as the Spirit enabled them" (Acts 2:4).

The Topeka event is commonly regarded as the beginning of the modern Pentecostal movement in America. Before the end of the century, it would involve over a half billion people in every corner of the world. In their special "Millennium" issue (Fall 1997), *Life* magazine listed the rise of the Pentecostal movement as sixty-eighth in their list of the one hundred most important events of the last thousand years.[8]

After Ozman experienced "tongues," Parham and the rest of the students sought and received the same experience.[9] Their experience was soon reported in the newspaper. Synan writes:

> In a short time the news of what was happening at "Stone's Folly" reached the press of Topeka and Kansas City. Soon reporters, government interpreters, and language experts converged on the school to investigate the new phenomenon. A few days later the *Topeka Capitol* reported in headlines. "A Queer Faith, Strange

Acts...Believers Speak in Strange Languages." The *Kansas City World* said "these people have a faith almost incomprehensible at this day."[10]

Visitors from the community began flocking to the Bible studies and prayer meetings to seek God for a similar experience, all of them hungry for whatever God had to offer. They not only received an ability to speak in a unique language, but they found new courage to tell others about Jesus Christ.

The Bethel Bible School did not reopen in the fall of 1901. Parham and many of the students scattered to the other communities. Parham loved street evangelism and praying for those who were ill or handicapped. As he was preaching in El Dorado Springs, Missouri, a woman named Mary Arthur was listening. She was legally blind and suffered from other ailments. Parham prayed for her, and she was dramatically healed. Mrs. Arthur quickly went home to Galena, Kansas, full of excitement and told her husband about her experience. He was amazed. His successful business career and financial security had not been of any help in healing his wife of her illness, but God had healed her supernaturally. Arthur quickly arranged for Parham to come to Galena.

The wire services picked up the story when Parham and his group of students visited Galena. Concerning this meeting, the *Cincinnati Enquirer* reported that it was doubtful that anything in recent years had awakened the interest, excited the comment, or "mystified the people" as had the events in Galena.[11] In 1903 and 1904 Parham preached to thousands in Galena, and many were converted to Christ, healed, and baptized in the Holy Spirit. Many took their experience to other cities and became lay preachers and evangelists, telling of a God who was active in the world today, just as He had been in the early church.

Parham then traveled to Houston, Texas, with twenty-four workers and started a Bible school, where they taught and preached about their new experience. William J. Seymour, a black holiness preacher who was blind in one eye, was among the small group of students in Houston. Later a small group of believers in Los Angeles invited Seymour to be their pastor and encourage them by preaching on holiness. Seymour accepted their invitation and began teaching about the baptism in the Holy Spirit according to Acts 2:4. Parham had convinced Seymour that God wanted this experience to be part of every Christian's life. This newly formed congregation did not expect that kind of doctrinal teaching, however, so they locked him out of the church. As a result, Seymour began prayer services in a home on nearby Bonnie Brae Street. During one of these services on April 9, 1906, seven people, including Seymour, received the baptism in the Holy Spirit and spoke in new languages.

As word began to spread, Seymour's group grew so quickly that he needed to find another building to house his followers. He found an old Methodist Episcopal church building at 312 Azusa Street. This forty-by-sixty foot, whitewashed, wood-frame structure soon accommodated as many as 350 people. A *Los Angeles Times* reporter visited the mission on April 17 and noted a "crowd" that included a majority of blacks with "a sprinkling of whites."[12] Outside the building several seekers, hecklers, and children were gathered. A. W. F. Manley reported in September 1906 that approximately three hundred whites and twenty-five blacks were present in the meeting he attended.[13] There was no question that something unique was happening on Azusa Street. God was doing a wonderful thing in people's lives, there were few, if any, racial barriers, and the gifts of the Holy Spirit were common.

Seymour's involvement in what is called the Azusa Street Revival was most certainly one of the most influential roles of any Christian leader in the twentieth century. The revival lasted for approximately three years. Night and day thousands of people from all over the country came to this humble building hungry for God. Many times they knelt through the night around the altar of that modest church repenting of their sins and seeking all that God had for them.

Seymour and others were criticized sharply for their insistence on "checking everything out with the Word."[14] But they were unashamed. In fact, Seymour responded to these criticisms in the September 1907 issue of *The Apostolic Faith:*

> We are measuring everything by the Word, every experience must measure up with the Bible. Some say that is going too far, but if we have lived too close to the Word, we will settle that with the Lord when we meet Him in the air.[15]

There is no way to know how many were affected by the revival at 312 Azusa Street. Theologian and church historian Stanley M. Horton says, "Multitudes came from every denomination to see what God was doing. Meetings continued every night, and the dawn often found a crowd still there praying for those seeking the baptism."[16]

The revival spread nationally and formed new congregations and transformed existing ones. The message spread internationally that God was touching lives in a new way with His Holy Spirit. People who had experienced the Azusa Street revival carried the message of the baptism in the Holy Spirit to Europe, China, the Philippines, Japan, Hong Kong, India, South Africa, Egypt, Liberia, and Canada.

This powerful fresh wave of enlightenment about the Holy Spirit transformed existing denominations and formed new denominations and church fellowships. Nearly every Pentecostal denomination in the United States and many throughout the world trace their roots to Azusa Street.

THE SPREADING FLAME

What began as a handful of believers at Stone's Folly in 1900 now has involved over a half billion people worldwide. At the turn of the century, less than 1 percent of the practicing Christians in the world were Pentecostal/charismatic. In the year 2000, 41 percent, or 562 million Christians will be Pentecostal or charismatic.[17] They will outnumber the combined total of sixty-one million Anglicans and 386 million Protestants.[18] With the projected rate of growth, it is anticipated that by 2025 one out of every two Christians worldwide will be Pentecostal or charismatic.[19] Harvard professor and theologian Harvey Cox writes:

> It is the fastest growing Christian movement on earth, increasing more rapidly than either militant Islam or the Christian fundamentalist sects with which it is sometimes confused. In Africa, Pentecostal congregations, usually called "African independent churches," are quickly becoming the main expression of Christianity. Several Latin American countries are now approaching Pentecostal majorities on a continent that had been dominated by Roman Catholicism for five centuries. The movement is growing in Korea and China.[20]

Russell Spittler of Vanguard University says, "We are headed for a 'third church' of the Southern Hemisphere that will be third-world in outlook and dominantly Pentecostal in religious style. Pentecostals form the new majority among Protestants."[21] Latin America has been experiencing revival for many years now. Numerous megachurches are popping up as revival sweeps across the continent. David Miller says:

> During the last decade, the population of Latin American Protestants increased by 220 percent, from 18.6 million to 59.4 million. Secular researchers report that four hundred Latin Americans convert to evangelical Christianity every hour. In Peru a new Protestant church is begun every eight hours and in Rio de Janeiro, one new congregation is planted every day. The fastest growth

has been in Pentecostal and Charismatic congregations, with 66 percent of Latin American Protestants attending a Pentecostal church.[22]

The twentieth century has seen the greatest outpouring of God's Spirit since the beginning of the church two thousand years ago. What a day to be alive!

Chapter 2

THE BLESSING:
THE BAPTISM OF THE HOLY SPIRIT

CHARLES FINNEY WRITES in his memoirs about a remarkable experience that made him one of the most powerful communicators of the gospel in his day:

I received a mighty baptism of the Holy Ghost. Without any expectation of it, without ever having the thought in my mind that there was any such thing for me, without any recollection that I had ever heard the thing mentioned by any person in the world, the Holy Spirit descended upon me in a manner that seemed to go through me, body and soul. I could feel the impression, like a wave of electricity, going through and through me. Indeed it seemed to come in waves and waves of liquid love; for I could not express it in any other way. It seemed like the very breath of God. I can recollect distinctly that it seemed to fan me, like immense wings.

No words can express the wonderful love that was shed abroad in my heart. I wept aloud with joy and love; and I do not know but I should say, I literally bellowed out the unutterable gushings of my heart. These waves came over me, and over me, one after the other, until I recollect I cried out, "I shall die if these waves continue to pass over me." I said, "Lord, I cannot bear any more," yet I had no fear of death.

How long I continued in this state, with this baptism

continuing to roll over me and go through me, I do not know. But I know it was late in the evening when a member of my choir, for I was the leader of the choir, came into the office to see me. He was a member of the church. He found me in this state of loud weeping, and said to me, "Mr. Finney, what ails you?" I could make him no answer for some time. He then said, "Are you in pain?" I gathered myself up as best I could, and replied, "No, but so happy that I cannot live."[1]

Finney continues:

"Now after receiving these baptisms of the Spirit I was quite willing to preach the Gospel. Nay, I found that I was unwilling to do anything else. I had no longer any desire to practice law."[2]

I believe Finney would agree with Pentecostal theologian J. Rodman Williams's statement, "Baptism in water means literally to be immersed in, plunged under, and even drenched or soaked with water. In effect, to be baptized in the Holy Spirit is to be totally enveloped in and saturated with the dynamic Spirit of the living God."[3]

Recently I met a pastor who had the life-changing experience of being baptized in the Holy Spirit. During his many years of graduate education, he had been taught that the miracles, signs, wonders, and charismatic experiences recorded in the Gospels and the Book of Acts were only for the early church. He listened well to his life as a pastor. Even though he knew his professors were sincere, he felt something was missing from his Christian life and ministry. As he studied the Word and meditated on the powerful experiences found in the Book of Acts, he hungered to have the same kind of experiences the early church had.

One day this young pastor visited a Pentecostal church that he had been told was experiencing revival. He had had revivals at his church, but they had been scheduled and had concluded within three to four days. This revival had been going on for weeks. When he entered the sanctuary, it was packed full of people worshiping God. The choruses were beautiful, and they uplifted Jesus Christ. The message was delivered with excellence, but the response of the people was different from that to which he was accustomed. People not only received Christ as their Savior, but many were prayed for to receive healing and the baptism in the Holy Spirit. He heard people speak in other languages, and he watched as people were touched by the presence of God. He too became hungry for a unique touch from the Holy Spirit and desperately wanted whatever God wanted for him. As he left the service that night, in his heart he prayed, "God, I need more of You. I need all You have for me; I am dry, empty, and ready for this gift if it is for me."

A few days later, as this young pastor was pushing his cart down the aisle at the local supermarket, he sensed God's presence all around him as he had at the church he had visited. There was no question in his mind that God desired to do something in his life. He began to quietly pray, and the words that came out were in a language he had never learned. Such an overwhelming presence of God, resulting in an incredible desire to worship God and love people, came with the gift he had just received. The hunger in his heart was being fulfilled. This pastor is a different man today. He is a wonderfully excited man who is absolutely certain that the Holy Spirit gives the same gifts today as He did during the days of the early church.

Stories such as this can be repeated literally scores of times around the world. There is a growing hunger in many peoples' hearts for all God has for them. We have sensed a new anticipation and eagerness in peoples' lives for God's power and His charismatic gifts.

THE FATHER'S GIFT

We have always loved Christmas and the birthdays of our children. Watching their eyes light up as they open a gift my wife and I purchased for them has been a tremendous joy. Giving brings benefits to both the receiver and the giver. We feel appreciated when we receive something we have desired or needed; but possibly more than the gift, we enjoy having others communicate to us that they care.

Jesus addressed the giving nature of God when He asked, "Which of you fathers, if your son asks for a fish, will give him a snake instead? Or if he asks for an egg, will give him a scorpion? If you then, though you are evil, know how to give good gifts to your children, how much more will your Father in heaven give the Holy Spirit to those who ask him!" (Luke 11:11–13).

Jesus was not referring to our "born again" experience at the time when the Holy Spirit is imparted (John 3:3–8), because at the moment we become born again, the new believer is automatically indwelt by the Holy Spirit. (See Romans 8:9–10, 14–16; 1 Corinthians 6:19–20.) Jesus was speaking of another experience with the Holy Spirit—the "gift" of the baptism in the Holy Spirit.

God gave this powerful gift to the early church, and it is available to the church of this century. Through misunderstanding, misinterpretation of Scripture, and naïveté, countless people have missed this wonderful gift. Also, sadly, many Christians have not earnestly desired all that God has for them. The baptism in the Holy Spirit is for you and for me. It will help you be all that God wants you to be. God wants to give this gift to every believer who desires it.

If your employer offered you a new tool to do your job with less physical effort but more excellence and precision, would you take advantage of the offer? If a friend told you of the availability of a new program that has a great ability to assist people in their efforts to be better husbands, wives, and parents, would you be interested in the program? How about an offer of some way to improve your Christian witness or multiply your efforts for God's kingdom? God has offered you a gift that will give you greater *dunamis,* "mighty power," and it will release the power of the Holy Spirit in your life.

THE PATTERN OF PENTECOST

John the Baptist, whose baptism was limited to water, prophesied that Jesus would "baptize...with the Holy Spirit and with fire" (Matt. 3:11).[4] The Bible tells us that after Jesus' resurrection, He spent forty days instructing his followers about the kingdom of God. "On one occasion, while he was eating with them, he gave them this command: 'Do not leave Jerusalem, but *wait for the gift my Father promised,* which you have heard me speak about. For John baptized with water, bit in a few days you will be baptized with the Holy Spirit'" (Acts 1:4–5, emphasis added).

The baptism in the Holy Spirit was first experienced on the Day of Pentecost. Luke describes this event in Acts 2:1–4, "When the day of Pentecost came, they were all together in one place. Suddenly a sound like the blowing of a violent wind came from heaven and filled the whole house where they were sitting. They saw what seemed to be tongues of fire that separated and came to rest on each of them. All of them were filled with the Holy Spirit and began to speak in other tongues as the Spirit enabled them." The promised blessing for which they were told to wait had come!

When about 120 people (Acts 1:15) in the early church received this experience after the resurrection of Jesus Christ, they were mocked by observers who said they were drunk. (See Acts 2:13.) Others wondered what it meant when so many people were speaking in languages they had never learned, "We hear them declaring the wonders of God in our own tongues!"

(Acts 2:11). Concerning this experience, Billy Graham writes, "What a day it was! It is difficult for us to imagine, with our practical, earth-bound, scientific mentality, the amazing happening of that day."[5]

In response to the crowd's comments and questions, Peter preached the first known sermon after the resurrection of Jesus Christ. As a result, about three thousand people became Christians that day. In his sermon Peter explained that this experience was the fulfillment of what the prophet Joel had said would happen in the last days, "In the last days, God says, I will pour out my Spirit on all people" (Acts 2:17). Peter challenged the crowd to "repent and be baptized, every one of you, in the name of Jesus Christ for the forgiveness of your sins. And you will receive the gift of the Holy Spirit. The promise is for you and your children and for all who are far off—for all whom the Lord our God will call" (vv. 38–39).

Among many other truths, Peter said that this "promise" is "for all who are far off." We are those people of whom Peter was speaking. God never intended this experience to be for the early believers only. It is for us. All over the world today, millions of Christians are receiving the same gift Jesus' early disciples received.

The infilling of the Holy Spirit on the Day of Pentecost began to be a pattern for "Spirit baptism" thereafter. When we become Christians, we receive the Holy Spirit (John 3:3–6; 20:22) and become participants in the divine nature. (See 2 Peter 1:4.) However, when we are baptized with the Holy Spirit, we receive power to witness for Christ and work with greater effectiveness within the church and before the world. (Acts 1:8.) We receive the same divine anointing that descended upon Christ (John 1:32–33) and upon the disciples (Acts 2:4), enabling us to proclaim God's Word (Acts 1:8; 4:31) and work miracles. (See Acts 2:43; 3:2–8; 5:12–16; 6:8; 10:38.)[6] "Spirit baptism is 'distinct from conversion,'" Pentecostal theologian Robert Menzies says, in that it "unleashes a new dimension of the Spirit's power: It is an enduement of power for service."[7] The giving of the Spirit is not for salvation but for greater service in God's kingdom.

It was critical that the disciples understood the purpose of the baptism in the Holy Spirit and that they not try to take any action to fulfill God's mission until they had received this experience. Jesus Christ himself did not begin His ministry until He was anointed with the Holy Spirit and power. (See Acts 10:38.) He instructed His disciples, "But you will receive power when the Holy Spirit comes on you; and you will be my witnesses in Jerusalem, and in all Judea and Samaria, and to the ends of the earth" (Acts 1:8). This experience would be God's most powerful gift.

Russell Spittler of Vanguard University accurately states, "Pentecostals would say: (1) Jesus was resurrected; (2) in the days that followed, He issued the great commission, but also, in Luke 24:49, told His disciples to wait in Jerusalem for the Holy Spirit; and (3) the Spirit came as Jesus promised, and the mission began."[8]

God desired each believer in Christ to be dynamically empowered by the Spirit. This experience does not make a Christian "more special" to God, because God does not show favoritism. However, the baptism in the Holy Spirit will give you greater boldness, along with a measure of power equal to the power that dwelt in the early believers. The person who receives this power will be able to accomplish marvelous works for God's kingdom. In your workplace, your marriage, your friendships—in difficulties, in spiritual battles, and in situations where you think you will not have the strength to go on, God will supernaturally enable you to be what you need to be and do what you need to do. This supernatural power is manifestation that comes with the blessing.

God wants His church to operate in supernatural power, not natural strength. The ultimate need is for every Christian to be supernaturally empowered so that the church will operate in the greatest possible dimension of life in the Spirit. Unaided human power to do the work of God is never enough. Paul reminded Timothy that the Holy Spirit is the "spirit of power" (2 Tim. 1:7). Paul also prayed for the Ephesian Christians that God would "strengthen you with power through his Spirit" (Eph. 3:16). Writing of his preaching to the Corinthian church, Paul said, "My message and my preaching were not with wise and persuasive words, but with a demonstration of the Spirit's power, so that your faith might not rest on men's wisdom, but on God's power" (1 Cor. 2:4–5).

This supernatural power explains how and why the early church was able to do the amazing work it did. Ordinary people spoke with power and saw tremendous results because the Holy Spirit was working in their lives. The wonderful truth is that when we read about how the early church operated, we can assume that we can be given the might to operate and function in similar ways. The manifestations of the early Christians can be our manifestations. The miracles they saw can be a part of our experience. The boldness that came to these early Christians can be ours as well.

BOLDNESS UNDER PRESSURE

I heard the story of a tremendous miracle that has affected literally thousands of people. Since the end of the Vietnam War there have been numerous efforts from various missions agencies to reach that country with the gospel of Jesus Christ. Because of God's help in these efforts, wonderful things have been happening. Many new churches have been started, orphanages have been built, and dynamic national people have come into leadership. Along with this, there has been great persecution and pressure to stop any attempt to evangelize the country, especially in the north.

In 1994 the Moses Caos family spoke in a worship service in Fresno, California, about their concern and burden for Vietnam.

As the service was ending, the people gathered around the Caos family and prayed for them.

During the prayer time, something amazing happened. A woman in the audience spoke out loud in the Vietnamese language. This woman had never learned that language, nor did she have any idea that she was speaking Vietnamese. The Caos family easily understood what she was saying.

As the woman began speaking, she spoke in the dialect of South Vietnam. Her words were words of encouragement and promises of God's faithfulness to the Caos family. The woman then began to speak in the dialect of North Vietnam. She cried out for the gospel to be preached in North Vietnam as well. She pled that the people in that part of the country would be able to hear the story of Jesus Christ, too.

Since that incredible event, hundreds of people from northern Vietnam have been responding to the gospel. There have been wonderful reports of healings, deliverances, and miracles. Also, many believers in Vietnam have been persecuted terribly and even imprisoned because of their faith.

This message in tongues given by the woman in Fresno was a great encouragement to those suffering in the north. Because of this demonstration of a supernatural gift, they know that God's heart yearns for them and that He is aware of all they are going through.[9]

The Holy Spirit's power was demonstrated in two major ways on this occasion. The woman had the ability to speak in a language she had never learned. (We will discuss this gift in more detail later in the book.) And she had the courage to speak out loud to the church and try to communicate what her spirit was feeling.

In turn, the Caos family was tremendously encouraged to spread the word back to their own country. God's use of a supernatural manifestation helped the Christians in northern Vietnam, and they became bolder in their faith.

The power that comes into Christians' lives when they

receive the baptism in the Holy Spirit enables them to do the work of God in spite of the difficulties and pressures they may encounter. It also helps them to be witnesses.

The Greek word for witness in *martyr*. Martyrs are willing to give up their lives for what they believe in. They are willing to die for their faith—millions have—because their convictions are strong. Seldom would the average person be willing to die for what he or she believes. Our Christian convictions need to be so strong that we are willing to give our very lives for the sake of the kingdom of God.

COMPELLED BY GOD

Those who have received the baptism in the Holy Spirit often feel compelled by God to say and do things and to enter occupations that they would not naturally seek. I did not want to go into the ministry, even though I had grown up in a minister's home. My father insisted that I go to a Bible college so, reluctantly, I did. I did not fit in. I was not happy because I was not living for God. I did not have the same commitment that I saw in my parents, and I avoided an unconditional surrender of my life to God. Then one day I felt that the Spirit of God touched my life. My heart melted from its stubbornness, and I felt convicted about not wholeheartedly serving Christ. I decided to yield my entire life to the Lord. From that day until now, I have only wanted to do what the Holy Spirit has told me to do. My experience is not unusual, because God has continually influenced people to change their goals, plans, and dreams in this way.

Missionary William Carey planned to go to the Great Polynesia in the South Seas. The Holy Spirit guided him to India, where he translated the Bible into nearly forty different languages and dialects. David Livingstone's ambition was to work in China. The Holy Spirit led him to Africa, where he became a missionary, statesman, and explorer. Adoniram Judson's choice was India. The Holy Spirit urged him to go to Burma, where he did a great work for God, translating the Bible into Burmese.[10]

It is important that we understand how critical our obedience is to the leading of the Holy Spirit. As small children learn how to walk and then run, so it is with learning how to walk in the Holy Spirit. As we take our first step by faith, God will reveal the next. We can expect God to make clear what we should do. As the renowned minister and writer A. T. Pierson says, "How many secrets of leading are yet to be brought to light, thousands of God's servants having been forbidden of Him to follow out their plans, because He has had some unexpected open door of service to set before them! And how we need to trust Him for guidance and rejoice equally in His restraints and constraints; because if we had infinite wisdom and love to guide us, we should not by one hair's breadth change His perfect plan for our lives!"[11]

When we receive the baptism in the Holy Spirit, we also receive a unique ability to be a witness. This does not mean that you will be expected to go into full-time ministry. Many have misunderstood the Lord's intentions in their lives and have entered ministry thinking they were obligated because they had received a wonderful experience from God. The baptism in the Holy Spirit is for everyone, and will be a tremendous help to you no matter what your occupation, your location, or your age. You will sense a new strength, authority, and confidence to be a testifier and communicator of God's truth about His precious Son Jesus Christ. The new millennium church of the twenty-first century, like the church in the Book of Acts, needs the dynamic power of the Spirit to equip it to evangelize the world and build the body of Christ. The Spirit came on the Day of Pentecost because Jesus' followers "needed a baptism in the Spirit that would empower their witness so that others might likewise enter into life and salvation."[12]

Each one of us needs the Holy Spirit's power. Anglican scholar

Henry Barclay Swete said, "As the whole church is consecrated for its spiritual priesthood by the gift of the Spirit, so the ministry of the church, which is directly concerned with spiritual things, needs in a high degree the anointing of the Spirit."[13]

COMMON CHARACTERISTICS OF SPIRIT-BAPTIZED CHRISTIANS

Evangelistic zeal

Being full of the Holy Spirit and winning the lost go hand in hand. Around the world, especially in Latin America, Africa, Eastern Europe, and the Pacific Rim countries, it is expected that "Spirit-filled" Christians are witnesses for Jesus Christ. "One of the chief reasons for the existence of the Pentecostal movement is evangelism."[14] Pentecostals read the Book of Acts and believe that the gifts of the Holy Spirit are available for them today. They observe that the early church was focused on evangelism and believe they must behave and respond in the same way. Evangelism is their primary goal. Because of this focus, Pentecostal missions programs have dynamically entered unconverted areas of the world, often at great risk, believing God would enable them to reach these areas for Christ.

Reliance on the Holy Spirit

Those who have been baptized in the Spirit have a unique experience with the Holy Spirit and rely on the Spirit's power and person. Larry Christenson, a leader in the Charismatic Renewal movement, says, "Pentecostal Christianity does not merely assume the presence and activity of the Holy Spirit in the church. It expects it, plans for it, and depends upon it."[15] And former general superintendent of the Assemblies of God Thomas F. Zimmerman once said, "Though we have grown in number, it would be foolish for us to assume that 'having begun in the Spirit' we could ever substitute mass strength for the power and presence of God in our lives. Our strength is not by might, nor by power, but by my Spirit, saith the Lord of hosts."[16] As the early church depended on the Holy Spirit to lead them in all they did and to give them the charismatic gifts necessary for the job, they believed that they would receive all the power they needed. When you have received the baptism in the Holy Spirit, you will have a similar dependency. You will assume that the Holy Spirit will help you in the same way He did the early church.

A unique power given by the Holy Spirit

Those who have received the baptism in the Holy Spirit believe a unique (not natural) dynamic power will be available to them as they do the will of God. Their "theology of power" has led to what some call "Supernatural evangelism."[17] In his book *Azusa Street and Beyond*, Grant McClung Jr. writes:

> For Pentecostals, every healing, miracle, spiritual manifestation, is a witness and testimony to the power of God. Healing lends value to conversion and becomes, in a sense…an earnest of the heavenly kingdom.…Signs and wonders become evangelistic means whereby the message of the kingdom is actualized in "person-centered" deliverance.
>
> Besides this, Pentecostals were willing to tackle "the dark side of the soul" and challenge the growing phenomenon of occultism, Satan worship, and demon possession. This head-on tackling of the enemy's power has become known in missiological circles as the "power encounter," a dynamic confrontation between two different and opposite religions in which the two are pitted against each other in open confrontation in Pentecostal missionary literature, and form a central part of Pentecostal missions strategy.[18]

Lay leadership

God greatly uses people who are not "professional clergy." The ability to be used by God is for everyone, not just those who are professionals. Worldwide, the Pentecostal/Charismatic church is growing largely because laypeople realize the gifts of the Holy Spirit are available to them. This realization enables them to take their personal experience with the Lord to their friends, family members, and acquaintances. They pray for and witness to others and ask God to perform healings and deliverances just as their pastors do. They depend on the Holy Spirit to lead them in their relationships, neighborhoods, and workplaces. Countless examples can be given about how "Spirit-baptized" congregation members have demonstrated gifts that many believe are available only to the clergy. Just as God used seven laymen in the early church, he will use laymen and laywomen today. (See Acts 6:1–6.)

A sense that Jesus Christ is actively involved in one's life

Those who have been baptized in the Spirit quite literally believe that Jesus will go with them to the ends of the earth. They anticipate that this power and authority will be available to them as they remain in right relationship with Him, live the Christian life, and witness to people who come across their paths. This understanding has greatly encouraged the typical Spirit-filled Christian to believe that Jesus will give him or her the gifts of the Holy Spirit just as He gave these gifts to the early church.

When we read about the experiences of those in the early church, we become hungry to be used of God in the same way. People were coming to Christ from all walks of life. God was powerfully using this small group of believers to break through the powers of darkness with signs and wonders. People were healed, delivered, and wonderfully transformed as the gospel spread throughout the land. You can be used in the same way. All around you are desperate, hurting, and confused people. Your Christian witness and life of faith demonstrated by the power of the Holy Spirit could be the very things that cause others to want what you have.

THIS GIFT IS PROMISED TO YOU

I often have felt that I needed every bit of the power available from God to do what he asks me to do. I cannot imagine not having the promised experience of the Holy Spirit. Hundreds of millions of people have received it. Joel prophesied that this gift would be given to the "last days" church (Joel 2:28; Acts 2:17), and Peter told the crowd who gathered on the Day of Pentecost that if they surrendered their lives to Jesus Christ, the promise was for them and their children and "for all who are far off—for all whom the Lord our God will call" (Acts 2:39).

I feel there is a good possibility that when we get to heaven we will be asked some questions. Two of them could be, "Did you receive the gift?" "What did you do with it?" Millions will say something like this, "I received the wonderful gift of the baptism in the Holy Spirit. Thank you for the supernatural strength to be a witness for Jesus Christ." Millions will also say, "I did not know it was for me. I thought it was only for special people like the apostles or the first Christians. How could I have missed it? I could have done so much more for the Lord if I had received this power."

How about you? Have you received the gift? If you have, what are you doing with it?

Chapter 3

THE EVIDENCE:
SPEAKING IN TONGUES

T HE AEGEAN SEA island of Patmos is a desolate and bar-
ren place about ten miles long and six miles wide. The
Romans used the island as a place to banish criminals.
The apostle John was sentenced to this island because of his
Christian faith.

George, a Greek immigrant to the United States, was born
on the isle of Patmos and values his Greek heritage and language. As an elder in a nominal church in Washington D. C.,
he became discouraged in his faith and disappointed by his
church. One Sunday morning Eva, his wife, asked him if he
would like to attend another church. The other church was a
strong, vibrant, Pentecostal church in the city, and she thought
that attending another type of worship service might be an
encouragement to her husband. George agreed. They enjoyed
their visit that day and decided to continue attending. The
teaching was solid, the people were encouraging and friendly,
and they felt at home. They did not, however, completely
understand the teaching on the gifts of the Holy Spirit.

After a Wednesday night Bible study when many were praying, George heard a familiar language. He said, "As I listened,
I could hardly believe my ears. Someone was speaking Greek
words—the language of my native Patmos!" When the prayer
time was over, George quickly went to the man you had been
speaking Greek.

"Where did you learn to speak Greek?" George asked the gentleman.

"I don't know a word of Greek," the man replied. "I began praying in this language when I received the baptism in the Holy Spirit."

George began weeping, praying, and thanking God that he would be interested enough in him to show him that the gifts of the Spirit are real. He and Eva were now convinced that God's gifts are for the church of today, not just for the early church.

Soon after this experience, George and Eva received the baptism in the Holy Spirit themselves and spoke in a language they had never learned.[1]

Missionary Denny Miller tells a similar story. He and his wife, Sandy, are missionaries to Malawi. One evening, after preaching in the village of Mtengo, Wathenga, many were praying around the front of the church. As Denny was praying with several of the people, he came upon a very old Malawian woman who was praising God in excellent English. The missionary naturally thought she knew English and prayed for her in English assuming she would understand. The local pastor pulled the missionary aside and said, "She has never spoken a word of English before." She had just been filled with the Spirit, and English was the language she had been given.[2]

These stories might seem unusual to you, or perhaps you are somewhat skeptical when you hear of people speaking in languages they have never learned. Speaking in tongues has been the subject of many discussions and the topic of many sermons. It is an experience shared by literally tens of millions of Christian people around the world. When asked, those Christians who speak in languages they have never learned will often say that they received the gift when they experienced being baptized in the Holy Spirit and then began using the language from that time on.

JERUSALEM OUTPOURING

We do not know the exact location in Jerusalem where the early disciples first received the baptism in the Holy Spirit.[3] We know that it was a large room because there were over a hundred people present. Probably the building was a typical Jerusalem structure made from stone, with mud for mortar. Most certainly, if everyone began praying out loud, the noise would have been heard by those nearby. Neighbors may have thought, *There is some kind of party or celebration going on over there.*

The Bible tells us that about 120 early disciples were together in one place (Acts 2:1) waiting for the "gift from the Father" (Acts 1:4) that Jesus had told them about. They did not know what that gift would be like, for Jesus had only said, "In a few days you will be baptized with the Holy Spirit" (Acts 1:5).

We can only speculate about how these early believers waited. I am sure there were prayers and many conversations asking, "When will the gift come?" and "What will it be like?" They certainly never doubted that there would be some show of God's power, for Jesus had promised it and had asked them to wait. Most of this crowd had seen the resurrected Jesus, and some had actually watched Him ascend into the clouds. Because of their firsthand experiences, the lives of these first followers of Jesus Christ would never be the same.

A sense of expectation filled the room. Although these believers were thoroughly convinced that something good was going to happen and that it was a promised gift from God, they probably had no idea exactly what they were anticipating or the possible physical impact or emotional feeling that would accompany it. They may have pondered and discussed the words of the prophet Joel:

> In the last days, God says, I will pour out my Spirit on
> all people. Your sons and daughters will prophesy, your
> young men will see visions, your old men will dream

> dreams. Even on my servants, both men and women, I will pour out my Spirit in those days, and they will prophesy.
>
> —ACTS 2:17–18

The believers knew that whatever the gift was, it must be important because Jesus was emphatic that they wait for the experience before they attempted to be "witnesses...to the ends of the earth" (Acts 1:8).

In his book *They Speak With Other Tongues*, John Sherrill makes these helpful comments:

> In both the Old and New Testaments the concept of power and Spirit are closely allied. In the Old Testament the power operates principally through great kings and prophets who lead the nation. In the New Testament the power is now about to be bestowed on the ordinary people who follow Christ.
>
> In both Testaments, when the Spirit touches human life, personality is transformed.[4]

Luke tells the account like this, "When the day of Pentecost came, they were all together in one place. Suddenly a sound like the blowing of a violent wind came from heaven and filled the whole house where they were sitting. They saw what seemed to be tongues of fire that separated and came to rest on each of them. All of them were filled with the Holy Spirit and began to speak in other tongues as the Spirit enabled them" (Acts 2:1–4).

Imagine it! The room filled with loud noise like that of a "violent" wind. This was not a storm hitting Jerusalem; the rest of the city was calm. The unexpected force was not natural; it was supernatural. Along with this loud noise, a wonderful presence of God must have filled the room—a feeling of great peace, contentment, and joy accompanied by amazing power and authority. Those present could physically and emotionally sense the Comforter. As the believers looked around at one another, they actually saw something like "fire" settle on each person in the room. Soon one, then another, then another began speaking in languages they had never learned. They must have been elated. "This is it! Finally, the *gift* Jesus promised!" Deep satisfaction and boldness began to fill their hearts as the experience continued on and on that Pentecost morning. No one had to explain what was happening. All of them were sure that the promised gift they had been waiting for had arrived.

There was a great deal of excitement in the room, and the noise could be heard outside. Others stopped and listened in amazement. They knew that the room was full of Galileans, but they heard them speaking in a variety of languages, "declaring the wonders of God" (Acts 2:11).

A crowd of onlookers began to gather outside the building, some mocking what was happening, and some sincerely wondering what it all meant.

John Sherrill writes:

> There was a quality about the experience that produced two responses. In the first place there were tongues. And then, at Pentecost, anyway, they got a little rowdy, enough so that the people watching wondered if they were drunk. It struck me as a curious contrast with the sobersided pulpits of today that the first Christian sermon should begin with a stout denial by the preacher that he and his friends were drunk. Why, he said, it is only nine in the morning, how could anyone be drunk?[5]

Stanley Horton notes:

> As soon as they were filled, the 120 began to speak (and continued speaking) with other tongues (languages). "Began" is significant in that it shows, as in Acts 1:1, that

35

what was begun was continued on other occasions, thus indicating that tongues were the normal accompaniment of the baptism in the Holy Spirit. This speaking came as the Spirit gave them utterance (proceeded to give and kept on giving them to utter forth or speak out). This is, they used their tongues, their muscles. They spoke, but the words did not come from their minds or thinking. The Spirit gave them the utterance, which they expressed boldly, loudly, and with obvious anointing and power. This was the one sign of the baptism in the Spirit that was repeated.[6]

When Peter decided to speak to the crowd, he had no doubt about what was going on. He gathered the other eleven apostles, and they were together as Peter preached his first sermon.

The phrase "Peter stood up" indicates that something dynamic had happened to him, for not many weeks before this experience, Peter had called down curses on himself and had sworn that he was not a follower of Jesus. (See Mark 14:71.) He had been afraid and had not wanted to associate with Jesus because he was on his way to a possible death sentence. In his mind Peter must have been tormented. His best friend was being taken away, and if he spoke up in his behalf, he would probably receive the same treatment. Perhaps his thoughts cried out, *I want to defend him! I need to say something! But if I do, they will take me too.* Because of his fear, Peter hastily denied it when someone recognized him, saying, "This fellow is one of them" (Mark 14:69).

But not now. This time "Peter stood up." He had another chance, and along with it he had a unique boldness and power. The fear was gone.

Peter was dramatically different. He had always loved being with Jesus. In fact, he had attempted things that none of the other disciples would attempt. When he and the disciples were crossing the Sea of Galilee, they had seen someone or something walking on the water:

When the disciples saw him walking on the lake, they were terrified. "It's a ghost," they said, and cried out in fear. But Jesus immediately said to them: "Take courage! It is I. Don't be afraid." "Lord, if it's you," Peter replied, "tell me to come to you on the water." "Come," he said.

—MATTHEW 14:26–29

Peter impulsively climbed out of the boat and began walking on the water toward Jesus thinking, *if the Lord tells me that I can do it, then I can,* and he did. When Peter suddenly realized what he was doing, he noticed the wind. Perhaps the waves and the spray of the water hit his body and he thought about the fact that he was walking on water. He began to sink. His faith had quickly turned into fear. The Bible says, "But when he saw the wind, he was afraid and, beginning to sink, cried out, 'Lord, save me!'" (Matt. 14:30).

Even though Peter was impetuous and the Lord saw and heard his denial, Jesus believed in him. In fact, his name was Simon, but Jesus renamed him Peter (Greek *Petros*), the rock. Jesus saw something in him that perhaps no one else saw—his potential.

Peter's experience reminds me of an event during an infamous Georgia Tech football game. A man named Roy Riegels recovered a fumble for California. Somehow Riegels became confused and started running sixty-five yards in the wrong direction. One of his teammates, Benny Lom, outdistanced him and tackled him just before he scored for the opposing team. When California attempted to punt, Tech blocked the kick and scored a two-point safety, which proved to be the ultimate margin of victory.

Those strange plays came in the first half, and everyone watching the game was asking the same question, "What will Coach Nibbs Price do with Roy Riegels in the second half?" The players filed off the field and went into the locker room and sat down on the benches and the floor—all but Riegels. He put his blanket around his shoulders, sat down in a corner, put his face in his hands, and cried like a baby.

A coach usually has a great deal to say to his team during halftime, but that day Coach Price was quiet. No doubt he was trying to decide what to do with Riegels. When the timekeeper came in and announced that there were only three minutes until game time, Price looked at the team and said simply, "Men, the same team that played the first half will start the second."

The players got up and started out—all but Riegels. He did not budge. The coach looked back and called to him again; still he did not move. Coach Price went over to where Riegels sat and said, "Roy, didn't you hear me? The same team that played the first half will start the second." Then Roy Riegels looked up, and Price saw that his cheeks were wet with a strong man's tears.

"Coach," he said, "I can't do it to save my life. I've ruined you. I've ruined myself. I couldn't face that crowd in the stadium to save my life."

Then Coach Nibbs Price put his hands on Riegel's shoulders and said, "Roy, get up and go on back. The game is only half over."

Riegels went back, and those Georgia Tech players will tell you they have never seen a man play football as well as Roy Riegels played in the second half.

Before Peter preached that first sermon, the Lord knew that Peter felt like a failure. But he also knew Peter would be different after he received the infilling of the Holy Spirit. He would no longer see waves, deny his Lord, or run because of fear. Instead, he would speak with boldness and power.

It is important for us to understand that Peter began his brief explanation of the upper-room experience with several references to Scripture. He did not say, "Look at this experience and what is happening to us. What is happening to us proves that what you see and hear is true." Just because a person has an experience does not make it truth. What makes an experience true is that it matches up with the Word of God.

Recently, at a large charismatic meeting, the speaker told the audience that they were not to question but accept what he was saying. This approach is not biblical; it is arrogant and of the flesh—or worse.

Peter's sermon was packed full of Scripture. He explained the experience of the 120 on the Day of Pentecost from Joel 2:28–32, then quoted Psalm 16:8–11 and 110:1 to establish how God fulfilled his promises in raising Jesus from the dead. If we cannot accept Jesus' work without finding it based on the written Word, how much more should we not accept anything a modern teacher says when it is not written in the Bible. Jesus himself resisted Satan by saying, "It is written" (Matt. 4:4).

Peter also did not focus his message on the experience of the infilling of the Holy Spirit. After briefly explaining from Scripture what had happened to the believers, he did exactly what Jesus said his followers would do after receiving the infilling—he became a powerful witness. Peter authoritatively preached about the life, death, resurrection, and exaltation of Jesus Christ. He said, "What you now see and hear" is the promised Holy Spirit the exalted Jesus has received from the Father. (See Acts 2:31–33.)

Not many days before and only a few blocks way, Peter had watched as Jesus was arrested by a crowd armed with swords and clubs. Once fearful, Peter now faced the crowd and said:

> "Therefore let all Israel be assured of this: God has made this Jesus, whom you crucified, both Lord and Christ." When the people heard this, they were cut to the heart and said to Peter and the other apostles, "Brothers, what shall we do?" Peter replied, "Repent and be baptized, every one of you, in the name of Jesus Christ for the forgiveness of your sins. And you will receive the gift of the Holy Spirit. The promise is for you and your children

> and for all who are far off—for all whom the Lord our
> God will call."
>
> —ACTS 2:36–39

As Peter spoke, his listeners "were cut to the heart." The Holy Spirit cut through their hardness, their resistance, and their mocking. This is the only place this phrase is used in the New Testament, but in the Old Testament Greek translation it is used in Genesis 34:7 to describe how the sons of Jacob felt when they discovered their sister, Dinah, had been raped by Shechem. Literally the phrase means, "to prick with a sharp point, to give a sharp pain associated with anxiety or remorse."

The crowd who was listening to Peter had all their emotional and mental barriers broken down by the Holy Spirit. They realized that what Peter was saying was true, and they wanted both to be relieved of conviction and to experience what had happened to the "upper-room" disciples.

They said, "What shall we do?"

Peter told them, "Repent." Take responsibility. Change your mind. Quit the blame game. "Be baptized, every one of you, in the name of Jesus Christ for the forgiveness of your sins." Forgiveness of sins comes with inner and outer obedience. Then "you will receive the gift of the Holy Spirit" (Acts 2:38). Why would they receive it too? Because it was God's promise. Since there are no second-class citizens in God's kingdom, the experience they had seen and heard could happen to them. Finally, Peter pleaded with them, warning, "Save yourselves from this corrupt generation" (Acts 2:40).

We do not know how long it took, but the events following Peter's sermon must certainly have gone on for hours. We can only imagine the sequence of time. A huge crowd made the decision that Peter's message was right and that the experience they had observed was authentic. They responded to Peter's appeal by accepting his message about Jesus Christ and by being baptized. In a day's time the church added about three thousand believers.

From that day Peter would never be the same. He had received the promise of the Holy Spirit, and with it he received the ability to speak in another language and God-given courage in his life.

THE EVIDENCE: THE HOUSE OF CORNELIUS

What was the evidence that Peter and the 120 had received the promised gift? Not only did they feel a unique boldness (defined as an emotional and dynamic courage to witness), but they spoke in another language (Greek *glossolalia* is translated "tongues" and is from the words *glossa*, meaning "language," and *ialia*, meaning "to speak"). This was something that was both observed and heard at the house of Cornelius. This realization later became the proof that the Gentile believers in the house of Cornelius had received eternal life too. "The gift of the Holy Spirit had been poured out even on the Gentiles. For they heard them speaking in tongues and praising God" (Acts 10:45–46).

Please do not misunderstand what we are saying. You do not have to speak in tongues to become a Christian. Your salvation is given to you because of your faith in the resurrected Christ, and by choosing to make Him the Lord of your life. (See Romans 10:9–10.) Your salvation has nothing to do with whether or not you speak in tongues; however, the baptism in the Holy Spirit with the ability to speak in tongues happens only to believers. We are saying that when the apostles found out that the Gentiles began speaking in tongues after Peter preached to them, they understood this as evidence that they had received the same baptism in the Holy Spirit that the 120 had received on the Day of Pentecost. And if they received this Holy Spirit baptism, they must be Christians, because only Christians receive this experience.

SAMARIA

The Bible tells us that "great persecution broke out against the church at Jerusalem, and all except the apostles were scattered throughout Judea and Samaria" (Acts 8:1). Philip was one of the early leaders and went to Samaria and began preaching about Christ. If there had been television cameras or newspapers then, they likely would have been reporting events that were happening concerning Philip, for he was greatly used of God to perform miraculous signs. Demon-possessed people were set free, and paralyzed and crippled people were healed of their infirmities. As a result of Philip's preaching, with signs and wonders following, many people converted to Christianity and were baptized in water.

This tremendous news reached the apostles in Jerusalem. When they heard that many in Samaria had accepted the word of God, Peter and John were sent to them to teach the new believers and to pray for them. The Bible tells us that when Peter and John arrived, "they prayed for them that they might receive the Holy Spirit, because the Holy Spirit had not yet come upon any of them" (Acts 8:15–16). Though the Samaritans had been baptized in water and in the name of the Lord Jesus, none had received the gift of the Spirit with the evidence of speaking in other tongues. That is, the Spirit had not come on any in the way He had come on the believers on the Day of Pentecost.[7]

Peter and John were concerned that the Samaritan believers receive the same power that they had received on the Day of Pentecost. Their experience was not a one-time event that happened to only the 120. Peter said, "The promise is for you and your children and for all who are far off—for all whom the Lord our God will call" (Acts 2:39). Peter and John then "placed their hands on them, and they received the Holy Spirit" (Acts 8:17).

How did the apostles know they had received the Holy

Spirit? Because they saw something happen. If the experience was only an inward quiet acceptance of the promise, nothing would have been seen.

Among the group in Samaria was a newly converted sorcerer named Simon. He was amazed by the powerful signs and miracles that were part of Philip's ministry. In fact, he wanted to buy this ability or learn how to reproduce it himself. "When Simon saw that the Spirit was given at the laying on of the apostles' hands, he offered them money and said, 'Give me also this ability so that everyone on whom I lay my hands may receive the Holy Spirit'" (Acts 8:18–19). Simon had seen something happen.

The issue is sometimes brought up that speaking in tongues is not mentioned in regard to the Samaritan believers receiving the baptism in the Holy Spirit, so therefore, tongues is not always the evidence of the experience. Theologian Stanley Horton makes this observation about the author of Acts, "Luke often does not explain everything when it is clear elsewhere. For example, he does not mention water baptism every time he tells about people believing or being added to the church, but it is clear that the failure to mention this is not significant. Other places show that all believers were baptized in water. For this reason we can say that the fact Luke does not mention speaking in tongues here is not significant."[8]

The context of the Book of Acts concerning speaking in tongues indicates that the apostles assumed that people who had received this experience demonstrated the initial evidence of *glossolalia;* they spoke in languages they had not previously learned. Whether speaking in tongues was the initial outward evidence was not even questioned in the early church. In fact, it was assumed that people who had received the Spirit baptism also received this ability. There is no record of this point even being an issue. Had it been a point of contention, it seems that Paul would have discussed it in his teaching on the subject in his Corinthian letter, in which he gave so much instruction on tongues. Since it was clearly understood, there was no need to make an issue of it. For this reason, it was not necessary for Luke, the companion of Paul and the early church historian, to mention this manifestation specifically each time someone or a group received the outpouring of the Holy Spirit.

F. F. Bruce agrees in his comments concerning the experience of the Samaritans, "The context leaves us in no doubt that their reception of the Spirit was attended by external manifestations such as had marked His descent on the earliest disciples at Pentecost."[9]

Peter immediately rebuked Simon for thinking he could buy the gifts of God for money and warned him to repent of his pride and trite view of God's power. What we need to comprehend is when the Samaritans received the Holy Spirit, something so evident happened that a former sorcerer wanted to know how he could do the same thing. In addition, Peter and John were satisfied that these new believers had received the same Holy Spirit they had received. We have no doubt that when Peter and John prayed for these young Christians, the Samaritans spoke in new languages just as those in the upper room on the Day of Pentecost; however, to come to this conclusion we must look at other groups who received this experience.

EPHESUS

Approximately twenty years after the initial outpouring on the Day of Pentecost, Paul encountered a group of believers in Ephesus.

Paul asked the disciples, "'Did you receive the Holy Spirit when you believed?' They answered, 'No, we have not even heard that there is a Holy Spirit'" (Acts 19:1-2).

The meaning of their answer does not seem to be that they had never heard of the existence of the Holy Spirit. A godly Jew or interested Gentile would not have been so ignorant. It is more likely that the phrase compares with John 7:39. There the phrase "By this he meant the Spirit, whom those who believed in him were later to receive" meant the age of the Spirit with its promised mighty outpouring had not yet come.[10]

From this we see that these Ephesian disciples were really saying that they had not heard that the baptism in the Holy Spirit was available.[11] In fact, several ancient manuscripts and versions of the New Testament actually read, "We have not even heard if any are receiving the Holy Spirit."[12]

Paul baptized these Ephesian disciples in water and then placed his hands on them. When he did this, they were baptized in the Holy Spirit. The same evidence given on the Day of Pentecost was given to them. "When Paul placed his hands on them, the Holy Spirit came on them, and they spoke in tongues and prophesied" (Acts 19:6).

PAUL

The apostle Paul was not in the Upper Room when the 120 were filled on the Day of Pentecost. At that time, he was a Jewish rabbi named Saul. He thought that those who followed Jesus were part of a growing sect. (See Acts 8:1–3; 9:1–2.) He was one of the greatest persecutors of the church until he had a dramatic experience with the Lord when traveling to Damascus. He was going to that city because he wanted to arrest those who "belonged to the Way" (Acts 9:2). As Saul neared Damascus, a light from heaven flashed around him. He fell to the ground with his eyes closed because of the brightness of the light. Jesus supernaturally revealed himself to Saul, and Saul in turn made Jesus Christ his Lord. When Saul stood and opened his eyes, he was blind. The blindness lasted for three days. Though he could not see the light of the sun or a candlelit room, a greater light came into his heart. He saw the resurrected Lord. His traveling companions led him by the hand into the city.

In Damascus there was a disciple named Ananias. When

Saul had been in the city for three days, Ananias had a vision. The Lord spoke to Ananias and told him where Saul was staying and instructed him to go to Saul. The Lord informed Ananias that he was to pray for Saul and his sight would be restored.

Saul was praying at approximately the same time. The Lord showed Saul in a vision that a man named Ananias would lay hands on him and pray for his healing. Scripture tells us, "Then Ananias went to the house and entered it. Placing his hands on Saul, he said, 'Brother Saul, the Lord—Jesus, who appeared to you on the road as you were coming here—has sent me so that you may see again and be filled with the Holy Spirit'" (Acts 9:17).

Immediately Saul was healed and was baptized in water and in the Holy Spirit. Many think that Saul could have been baptized in the Holy Spirit before he was baptized in water, as was the experience of Cornelius. There are similarities between the way God sent Ananias to Saul and the way he sent Peter to Cornelius. Stanley Horton remarked about this experience:

> Verse 12 does not tell the command of Jesus to lay hands on Saul that he might be filled with the Holy Spirit. Neither does verse 18 tell how Saul did receive the Spirit. Once again, we see that Luke does not repeat everything in every place. Thus, he really indicates that Saul's experience in being filled with the Holy Spirit was no different from that experienced on the Day of Pentecost. We can be sure he spoke in other tongues at that time, as they did in Acts 2:4.
>
> Titus 3:5–7 confirms this by showing that the Holy Spirit was poured out on both Saul and Titus abundantly. Each had his own personal Pentecost. Actually, there is really no question about whether Saul spoke in tongues or not. He told the Corinthians years later that he spoke in tongues more than them all. (See 1 Corinthians 14:18.)[13]

WHAT HAPPENS WHEN WE
SPEAK IN TONGUES?

Many sincere people have asked, "Why speak in tongues? What good will it do me?"

They might also say, "I can accept the idea that many Christian people pray in languages that they have never learned, and that this is a unique gift from God, but I like praying in my own language, and I do that often. Do I need a special prayer language?"

Another common question is, "If I have this gift but do not use it, does that mean that I am not serving the Lord as faithfully as I should?"

These are all good questions, and they deserve biblical answers. It is important for us to understand that our creator God knows what will benefit us and what will harm us. God would not have given this gift to the early church, nor would He give it to you, if there was any possibility that it would be a detriment to them or to you. In our spiritual pilgrimage, we need to know that our heavenly Father only wants to help us and benefit us in every way possible. Biblical scholar Gordon D. Fee feels that the Scripture outlines three benefits for those who have the gift of speaking in tongues:

1. Such a person is "speaking to God," that is, he or she is communing with God by the Spirit.... The tongues-speaker is not addressing fellow believers but God (1 Corinthians 14:13–14, 28), meaning therefore that Paul understands the phenomenon basically to be prayer and praise.

2. The content of such utterances is "mysteries" spoken "by the Spirit." It is possible that "mysteries" means something similar to its usage in 1 Corinthians 13:2; more likely it carries here the sense of that which lies outside the understanding, both of the speaker

and the hearer. After all, "mysteries" in 13:2 refers to ways of God that are being revealed by the Spirit to his people; such "mysteries" would scarcely need to be spoken back to God.

3. Such speech by the Spirit is further described in 1 Corinthians 14:4 as edifying to the speaker. This has sometimes been called "self-edification," and therefore viewed as pejorative. But Paul intended no such thing. The edifying of oneself is not self-centeredness, but the personal edifying of the believer that comes through private prayer and praise. Although one may wonder how "mysteries" that are not understood even by the speaker can edify, the answer lies in 1 Corinthians 14:14–15. Contrary to the opinion of many, spiritual edification can take place in ways other than through the cortex of the brain. Paul believed in the immediate communing with God by means of the Spirit that sometimes bypassed the mind; and in verses 14 and 15 he argues that for his own edification he will have both. But in church he will have only what can also communicate to other believers through their minds.[14]

Elaborating on Dr. Fee's comments, there are four additional benefits we want to point out:

1. Worship and praise

The gift of speaking in tongues will enable people to worship and praise God from the depths of their spirit. On the Day of Pentecost, the onlookers commented, "Are not all these men who are speaking Galileans?...we hear them declaring the wonders of God in our own tongues!" (Acts 2:7, 11). The word *wonders* comes from the original Greek word *megaleios*, which means "conspicuous, magnificent, splendid, majestic, sublime, grand, beautiful, excellent, favorable." The onlookers heard the disciples speaking in their own languages about the majestic greatness of God and His magnificent deeds. Giving thanks and praise to God is a wonderful habit to acquire. Christians who pray in their prayer language can know they are uplifting the Lord and offering heartfelt praise to Him.

2. Personal edification

Paul informs us that "he who speaks in a tongue edifies himself" (1 Cor. 14:4). All of us need personal edification. The edification that Paul mentions here is not arrogance, pride, or self-centeredness. It is a pure edification that strengthens and promotes our spiritual beings, encouraging maturity and godly characteristics in our lives. It will deepen our love for God, give us a greater concern for others, and encourage us to keep our hearts and consciences clean before the Lord. People often comment that when they pray in tongues, they feel encouraged and uplifted in the Lord. Very possibly the reason for this could be that they have been confessing the motives of their hearts and praying in the perfect will of God.

God wants everyone in the body of Christ to have every possible advantage in his or her Christian walk. He would like everyone to be able to have more edification and heaven-directed encouragement. Since God is no respecter of persons, we all are on equal ground. What benefits one can benefit another. This is one reason we believe speaking in tongues is available to everyone who receives the Spirit baptism.

3. Spirit prayer

First Corinthians 14:2 says, "For anyone who speaks in a tongue does not speak to men but to God. Indeed, no one understands him; he utters mysteries with his spirit." Pastor Jack Hayford explains that:

> Paul's assertion clearly establishes the primary purpose for tongues as the gift of the Spirit for private worship. It is a unique Godward and not manward gift.... Therefore,

they can take on a strictly spiritual form of expression, since man is not their goal. The seat of their operation is not the mind, but the spirit (1 Corinthians 14:14–15). They are an enablement of the Spirit for nonconceptual communication directly with God, who is Spirit (John 4:24). This is why they are so vastly important and constantly used by Paul. (See 1 Corinthians 14:18.) Mysteries, as elsewhere in the New Testament, refers to secrets which have been revealed.[15]

Often we cannot think of the words to say or cannot communicate to God thoroughly how we really feel about something. I recently heard of a person who had this kind of experience.

Over ten years ago, I performed a wedding in Bitburg, (then West) Germany. "Bob," the young groom, who had been part of a church I pastored, was in Germany in the U. S. Air Force. He had been an outstanding leader in our youth group, and continued to be faithful to the Lord while serving in the military. Bob met a wonderful Christian woman who was stationed in Bitburg. After dating for a while, they decided to marry. Bob heard that I was going to be speaking in Germany, so he and "Brenda" contacted me and asked if I would perform the wedding ceremony. I was honored to be a part of their celebration.

Not long after I returned to the States, Bob and Brenda, like many couples, realized they had tremendous differences, and both of them stubbornly held on to their opinions and ways of living. Over the years the friction developed into a tremendous division in their hearts toward one another. The arguing turned into yelling, name-calling, and saying things they regretted. Even though God gave them two beautiful children, they wondered if they should remain married. About this time Bob informed me that the marriage was in disarray. Several times we talked and prayed together about their desperate situation. I was greatly saddened and felt that without God's help this marriage was on its way to becoming another divorce statistic. I had not heard from Bob for a few days until just recently when he called me.

In our conversation I noticed that Bob was excited about how involved he had become in his community and his church. He was happy, motivated, and seemed strong in the Lord—like the "old Bob" I had known when he was in our church youth group. In the back of my mind, I wondered, *What about Brenda and the children? Where are they? When did the marriage end?*

Bob then added, "By the way, my marriage has never been better. Brenda and I have never gotten along so well, and our kids are doing super, too."

I was thrilled and quickly responded, "Tell me what happened."

"My relationship with Brenda is incredible in every way. We communicate better, our love for each other is greater, and we enjoy each other more than we ever could imagined," Bob responded.

"Bob, I couldn't be happier for you. I wondered what had happened with your life and your marriage," I said. "Many times I have thought of you and prayed for you. Tell me, was there any one thing you can point to that began to change your hearts and minds about each other?"

Bob answered, "Pastor, you might think this is strange, but I was so desperate and our marriage was so hopeless, that I couldn't pray in English about it anymore. I began crying out to God in tongues. Everyday I prayed in this language until I felt less burdened. I also started feeling differently about Brenda. I had compassion toward her and the kids and wanted to be a better husband and father. My attitude and outlook changed. Then my words and behavior toward her changed, too. After twelve years of marriage, it has never been better. I'm deeply in love with my wife again, and our family is doing great."

There is no question in my mind that Bob became so broken that he desperately cried out to God with his spirit in another tongue. Only God knows the confessions and spirit-felt prayers Bob prayed during those months. God did not want any marriage to have that kind of difficulty. I believe that Bob prayed during those months. God did not want Bob and Brenda's marriage to end, nor does he want any marriage to have that kind of difficulty. I believe that Bob was praying for the healing of his marriage, an attitude change, and for unique situations in his own life that only God knew about. His spirit prayed in ways that his mind never could have prayed.

Some have misunderstood and thought that persons need to go into some kind of meditative semiconscious state, similar to a yoga posture, before they are able to speak in tongues. This simply is not the case. Just as bilingual persons can begin speaking in another language "at will," so persons who have the gift of speaking in tongues can use this gift, or decide not to use it, whenever they wish. As Oswald Chambers once said, "The Holy Spirit does not obliterate a man's personality; He lifts it to its highest use."

Over the years we have been asked, "What about Billy Graham or someone else who has been greatly used of God? Has he ever had this experience?" Though we do not develop our theology from people's experiences, but only from Scripture, it is at times helpful to know the experiences of godly people. Specifically, we cannot accurately answer the question about Dr. Graham because we do not know. He has from time to time written or spoken about a deep experience with the Lord; however, he has chosen not to give great detail about these times. He has always been cautious to communicate and position himself in such a way that he would not offend any segment of the body of Christ. We have tremendous respect for Dr. Graham and feel that he has done much more for the kingdom than many who profess to have received the baptism in the Holy Spirit.[16] There is no question that God has gifted this man in unique and powerful ways. It is not a matter of comparison that once you have had the experience you are on a higher ground or are closer to the Lord—it is a matter of the raw material that is worked with. God fills whomever He chooses and gives those people greater power than they ever could have had naturally.

John Sherrill shares part of a letter he received from a psychiatrist concerning the power of the gift of praying in tongues:

> Each morning before the day's appointments begin my wife and I have prayer time together. We pray for our own needs and then for each patient I will see that day.... We mention first our own insights into his problem, using the notes I have made during his sessions, and what we know of medicine and psychiatry. But then, realizing how much of mental illness still defies understanding, we include a prayer for him in tongues. I am frequently astonished at the healing power that is present in sessions following these prayers.[17]

4. Sense of assurance

When we experience speaking in tongues, we have a sense of assurance that we have received the baptism in the Holy Spirit of which both Jesus and John the Baptist spoke. In times of doubt, we can remind ourselves that God gives this gift only to those who have been baptized in the Spirit. As the "stones" served as the reminder to the children of Israel that they finally crossed the Jordan River into the Land of Canaan (Josh. 4:1-7), so this experience with the gift of speaking in another language can remind us of what God did for us when we received the promised baptism.

THE PROMISE IS FOR YOU

As Peter finished his powerful message on the Day of Pentecost, he said, "The promise is for you and your children and for all who are far off—for all whom the Lord our God will call" (Acts 2:39).

What is the "promise"? It is the gift of the Holy Spirit. It is for you, your family, and anyone who is the body of Christ. The experience of the early church can be the same for you and me.

Why is it a language that we have never learned? The late Episcopalian pastor Dennis J. Bennett said:

> Speaking in tongues enables a person to speak or pray to God without interference from any human source, including himself; without the mind, emotions, or will intruding into the picture. The indwelling Spirit says in effect, "I know what you need to express to God the Father. Trust me to guide you as you speak." Thus confession can be made of sins that the mind does not even know about and would not acknowledge, or would soften and rephrase if it did. On the positive side, love for God can be expressed with a fullness and freedom otherwise impossible to the person because of inhibitions and fears of expression. Intercession can be made for others, expressing their deepest needs, without the intercessor knowing what these needs are.
>
> "We know not what we should pray for as we ought," says Paul, "but the Spirit itself maketh intercession for us...." *The Basic English New Testament* version of this quotation is "The Spirit puts our desire into words which are not in our power to say..."
>
> *The Living Bible* paraphrases it thus: "The Holy Spirit prays for us with such feeling that it cannot be expressed in words, and the Father, who knows all hearts, knows of course what the Spirit is saying as he pleads." Surely these describe speaking in tongues.[18]

Chapter 4

THE OVERFLOW: BEING FILLED WITH THE HOLY SPIRIT

T HE LAUGHTER OF children abruptly was silenced when the station wagon in which they were riding hit a trailer and they instantly passed from this life to the next. It had been raining off and on most of the day, and it was now dark on the highway to Tehran, Iran. Out of nowhere a loaded farm trailer had appeared on the highway, and the station wagon had slammed into the rear of it.

The two families in the station wagon had been traveling for about four hours and had decided to visit a Spirit-filled American couple. The conversation that late afternoon had been full of concern over the spiritual condition of the people in that area of Iran. They wept as they prayed together for God to touch that needy country. As they left, the families had no idea that tragedy would soon visit them.

The four adults in the car have no memory of the events just prior to the impact. The passengers were missionaries Mark and Gladys Bliss and their three children, thirteen-year-old Karen, eleven-year-old Gail, and three-year old Mark. Traveling with them were Iranian pastor Haik Hovsepian, his wife, and their three-month-old baby boy. All four children were killed. Shortly after the tragedy, an American doctor by the name of Dr. Briggs came upon the accident and was instrumental in saving the lives of the four injured adults. Gladys was unconscious with a fractured skull, shattered hip, and broken collarbone and jaw. Mark had three broken ribs and numerous cuts on his face and forehead. Pastor Haik and his wife both had broken legs.

Only days before, when young Karen had been leaving the school chapel, she had been asked by her teacher, "Why do you come out so early?" Karen said, "I have a longing in my heart to be as much like Jesus as possible, and I want to be alone to pray."

Vivacious and happy Gail loved people and loved life.

A friend remembers little Mark singing, "Praise Ye the Lord, Hallelujah!" and "Jesus Loves Me."

The news of the crash quickly traveled to other parts of the world, and the missionary organization immediately rallied around the Blisses. One missionary called the Tehran General Hospital from out of the country. When questioned about the children, Mark replied, "They are with the Lord. I think we will bury them here. I have great comfort and peace from the Lord. I trust my wife will receive the same." After surgery Gladys regained consciousness. She was told about her children and told that the head of the mission's agency was greatly concerned and had been calling. With quiet determination she said, "Tell him we are going to make it."

Later, at the funeral service, Mark said:

> If it had been one child, it would have been difficult. God's grace would have met us. But God in His plan has taken all three. I still testify to you that God's grace is sufficient. God is giving to my wife the same grace that He has given to me. I want to testify to His faithfulness. I have never before felt closer to the heart of God. In this hour, I feel His presence so real that I want to encourage you, my friends, who have been so kind in standing by us. God bless each one of you. God has blessed these three with the ultimate, the greatest blessing, for they are absent from the body and they are present with the Lord.[1]

Mark and Gladys decided to stay in Iran. Most would certainly have understood and even expected them to leave and go back to the United States and start over. The pain that comes with this kind of tragedy defies imagination, and it is common for a divorce to follow. They did not leave. They did not become bitter or resentful toward the country or the people of Iran because of the terrible road conditions and careless driver, and they did not even consider ending their marriage. In fact, the opposite happened. They stayed in Iran for another twenty-five years, a time when persecution grew more and more intense and life became very difficult for even the strongest people. They were involved in witnessing to countless people, and they depended on each other more than ever.

If you asked Mark and Gladys today, "Why did you stay?" or "How did you cope with such pain?" without hesitation they would answer that the love of God compelled them and the Holy Spirit strengthened them and helped them understand that, in spite of their precious human loss, the depth of spiritual need for the people of Iran was—and is—greater. The Holy Spirit helped them to see the people of Iran through the eyes of Jesus. After all, does Scripture not tell us that the Holy Spirit will take "from what is mine and make it known to you"? (John 16:15). Jesus died for the people of Iran, and Mark and Gladys Bliss were two of his ambassadors representing Him in that country. In spite of their inconceivable personal pain, Mark and Gladys were able to love the people of Iran and find an unequaled strength that could only come from the Holy Spirit.

There is no question that when people are full of the Holy Spirit they act, think, and treat people differently than others do. Those who think they can treat people badly or get away with consistently acting rude or arrogant need to understand that their behavior grieves the Holy Spirit. God is love, and we are to treat people as He does. God gave us the gifts of the

Holy Spirit, and it is necessary that we permit Him to use the gifts of the Holy Spirit, and it is necessary that we permit Him to use the gifts in our lives as we endeavor to reach this lost and dying world. More even than being used in the gifts, we need to demonstrate a Christlike life to those around us. Love is more important than any gift, but to love people the way God wants us to, we need the help of the Holy Spirit. Joseph Fletcher said, "Love is not the work of the Holy Spirit; it is the Holy Spirit—working in us. God is love. He does not merely have it or give it; He gives Himself—to all men, to all sorts and conditions."[2]

GOD IS LOVE

After Paul instructed the Corinthian believers about the gifts of the Holy Spirit (1 Cor. 12), and before he told them how the gifts are to be used in our private lives and in the church setting (1 Cor. 14), he wrote to them about love in chapter 13. The church in Corinth was known for its charismatic gifts. They had talented preachers come through town and saw tremendous miracles, but they had a spiritual pride about their abilities and an arrogance about their church that greatly irritated Paul. He basically said that he did not care how much ability they had or what "charisma" gifts they had, if they did not act like Christ and demonstrate love, they had nothing. Paul wrote:

> If I speak in the tongues of men and of angels, but have not love, I am only a resounding gong or a clanging cymbal. If I have the gift of prophecy and can fathom all mysteries and all knowledge, and if I have a faith that can move mountains, but have not love, I am nothing. If I give all I possess to the poor and surrender my body to the flames, but have not love, I gain nothing.
> —1 CORINTHIANS 13:1–3

The world might be impressed by our gifts, and those gifts might draw attention to us or to a certain church or crusade, but we must understand that what will win non-Christians more than anything else is when they see the love of God through our life and our words. As D. L. Moody said, "The churches would soon be filled if outsiders could find that people in them love them when they came. This love draws sinners! We must win them to us first, and then we can win them to Christ. We must get people to love us, and then turn them over to Christ."[3] When Christians are full of the Holy Spirit, they are full of God's love for people, and the Holy Spirit helps them live a life that will draw others to Christ. Henry Drummond said, "Real love is the universal language—understood by all. You may have every accomplishment or give your body to be burned; but, if love is lacking, all this will profit you and the cause of Christ nothing."[4]

I was recently traveling with a friend who kept talking about developing a program to help with the desperate needs of America's inner cities. The groups of people he wanted to help were being ignored by many. On and on the conversation went. He talked about the history of some of the problems inner-city people faced and about strategies he could develop. He kept coming up with new ideas and brainstormed with me about what he could do if he had the financial backing to pull it off.

I too felt this concern, but as I looked in his eyes and sensed the resoluteness in his heart, I could not help but notice that the subject was consuming him.

I asked him, "Why is this on your mind so much? Some of the things you are thinking about will take years to develop and the finances will be enormous. I'll help you in any way I can, but this will also take the financial backing of many others."

He said, "I can't get these people off of my mind. When I sleep I dream about them. When I'm awake I see their faces.

When I'm with them I weep with them. Their hardness toward life only makes me love them more."

I thought, *The love of God is filling this man's life with these people.*

We cannot understand God's love and compassion for humankind. People like Mark and Gladys Bliss and my friend are led by the Holy Spirit and will be given unique gifts to reach the group of people with whom they are concerned. Their compassion first started in the heart of God.

When David Wilkerson, the founder of Teen Challenge, went to New York City forty years ago, he went in response to a *Life* magazine story he had read about seven teenage gang members who had killed a fifteen-year-old polio-stricken boy named Michael Farmer. When David looked at the pictures of one of the young murderers, his eye caught a desperate look of despair and hatred. He began to cry and said to himself, "What's the matter with me?" A thought quickly came to his mind that seemed to come from somewhere else. "Go to New York City and help those boys."[5]

He left the hills of Philipsburg, Pennsylvania, where he was minister in a small community, and decided that he would try to help the kids of New York. David and his wife, Gwen, prayed that God would perform miracles in their behalf so they could reach the gang members they saw in the *Life* magazine picture and others like them.

One day David met the gang called the Mau Maus. In his book *The Cross and the Switchblade,* he writes:

> Israel, the president of the gang, was as nice a boy as I've met; he stuck out his hand and shook mine like a gentleman.
>
> Nicky was something else. I remember thinking, as I looked at him, that's the hardest face I have ever seen.
>
> "How do you do, Nicky," I said.
>
> He left me standing with my hand outstretched. He

wouldn't even look at me. He was puffing away at a cigarette, shooting nervous little jets of smoke out the side of his mouth.

"Go to Hell, Preacher," he said. He had an odd, strangled way of speaking and he stuttered badly over some of his sounds.

"You don't think much of me, Nicky," I said, "but I feel different about you. I love you, Nicky." I took a step toward him.

"You come near me, Preacher," he said, in that tortured voice, "I'll kill you."

"You could do that," I agreed. "You could cut me in a thousand pieces and lay them out in the street and every piece would love you."[6]

David did not realize it, but that statement cut Nicky to the core of his being. No one had ever loved him that way or even had said, "I love you" to him. Nicky was a hardened gang leader and a criminal. He could steal, lie, cheat, and even kill if necessary. But this little preacher from the hills of Pennsylvania got to him. In reality, the Holy Spirit helped David feel what he felt so he could say what he said. Soon after this meeting Nicky gave his life to Christ. He was baptized in the Holy Spirit, and throughout the following years he became a powerful evangelist who helps kids in the same condition he was once in. What won Nicky? It was the love of God.

MAKE GOD'S LOVE YOUR GOAL

In describing how we should love, Paul says, "Love is patient, love is kind. It does not envy, it does not boast, it is not proud. It is not rude, it is not self-seeking, it is not easily angered, it keeps no record of wrongs. Love does not delight in evil but rejoices with the truth. It always protects, always trusts, always hopes, always perseveres" (1 Cor. 13:4–7).

The Bible tells us that "God is love" (1 John 4:8), and the Spirit of God desires us to live a life of love. I like to think of the biblical definition of love and make it a goal to apply it to my life in this way:

- The Holy Spirit is patient, and He will help me to be patient with people and in various circumstances.

- The Holy Spirit is kind, and He will help me to be kind at all times no matter how someone has treated me or what people have said about me.

- The Holy Spirit does not envy, and He will help me not to envy those who have acquired much materially or achieved much in life or career.

- The Holy Spirit does not boast, and He will help me not to boast in my success or gain but to humbly recognize that "all good things" come from my heavenly Father above.

- The Holy Spirit is not proud, and He will help me not to be proud with the gifts God has given me or the accomplishments that He chooses to let come into my life.

- The Holy Spirit is not rude, and He will help me not to be rude to those I associate with in my family or my work, or to people of any race, color, culture, age group, or socio-economic class. He helps me understand that all people are created in the image of God and are on level ground.

- The Holy Spirit is not self-seeking, and He will help me not to be self-seeking but to passionately seek the will of God and to serve others.

- The Holy Spirit is not easily angered, and He will help me not to become easily angered when people say angry things to me or treat me unjustly or disrespectfully.

- The Holy Spirit keeps no record of wrongs, and He will help me not to keep an account of wrongs when others offend me, sin against me, gossip about me, or try to bring harm to my reputation.

- The Holy Spirit does not delight in evil, and He will help me not to be happy when bad things happen to other people no matter how harmful these people have been.

- The Holy Spirit rejoices in truth, and He will help me to be sincerely happy with the accomplishments, successes, and recognition that others receive when they do good things.

- The Holy Spirit always trusts, and He will help me trust and believe what is best about people around me.

- The Holy Spirit always hopes, and He will help me hope and pray for God's best in others' lives and not give up on them when it seems that everyone else has.

- The Holy Spirit always perseveres, and He will help me be patient with others knowing that none is perfect and all must work out their salvation with fear and trembling.

People who have been baptized in the Holy Spirit want to act like the Holy Spirit. They have been so immersed in the Holy Spirit that He is part of their every move and is involved in every relationship they have. They are sensitive to the things the Holy Spirit is sensitive to, and they care about what the Holy Spirit cares about. Our lives demonstrate whether we are full of the Holy Spirit or not.

There is no question that D. L. Moody was one of the most successful evangelists in history. Along with his successful campaigns, he developed a deep hunger for more of God and his power. He felt an increasing awareness of his own personal inadequacies to do the work God had called him to do and knew that he needed something more from God in order to accomplish all that was in his heart. This awareness was heightened one day when he spoke to two women who sat in the front pew of his church in Chicago.

Often at the close of a service, they would say to him:

"We have been praying for you."

"Why don't you pray for the people?" Moody would ask.

"Because you need the power of the Spirit," was the reply.

"I need the power! Why," said he in relating the incident afterward, "I thought I had power. I had the largest congregation in Chicago, and there were many conversions. I was in a sense satisfied. But right along those two godly women kept praying for me, and their earnest talk about anointing for special service set me thinking. I asked them to come and talk with me, and they poured out their hearts in prayer that I might receive the filling of the Holy Spirit. There came a great hunger into my soul. I did not know what it was. I began to cry out, as I never did before. I really felt that I did not want to live if I could not have this power for service."

"While Mr. Moody was in this mental and spiritual condition," says his son, "Chicago was laid in ashes. The great fire swept out of existence both Farwell Hall and Illinois Street Church. On Sunday night after the meeting, as Mr. Moody went homeward, he saw the glare of flames, and knew it meant ruin in Chicago. About one o'clock Farwell Hall was burned; and soon his church went down. Everything was scattered."

Mr. Moody went east to New York City to collect funds for the sufferers from the Chicago fire, but his heart and soul were crying out for the power from on high. "My heart was not in the work of begging," he said. "I could not appeal. I was crying all the time that God would fill me with His Spirit. Well, one day, in the city of New York—oh, what a day!—I cannot describe it. I seldom refer to it; it is almost too sacred an experience to name. Paul had an experience of which he never spoke for fourteen years. I can only say that God revealed Himself to me, and I had such an experience of His love that I had to ask Him to stay His hand. I went to preaching again. The sermons were not different; I did not present any new truths; and yet hundreds were converted. I would not now be placed back where I was before that blessed experience if you should give me all the world—it would be as the small dust of the balance."[7]

Moody wrote, "I never knew up to that time that God loved us so much. This heart of mine began to thaw out; I could not keep back the tears. I just drank it in. . . . I tell you there is one thing that draws above everything else in the world and that is love."[8]

D. L. Moody and many others have believed that when people see the love of God demonstrated in what we say and do, they will be drawn to what we have. In the personal notes of his Bible, Moody wrote:

> The fruits of the Spirit in terms of love:
> Joy is love exulting.
> Peace is love reposing.
> Long-suffering is love untiring.
> Gentleness is love enduring.
> Goodness is love in action.

Faith is love on the battlefield.
Meekness is love under discipline.
Temperance is love in training.[9]

THE FRUIT OF THE HOLY SPIRIT

Charles Spurgeon prayed, "Lord…make my inward grace to be so vigorous that my outer life may be fruitful to Thy praise."[10]

The Upas tree, which grows in Indonesia, secretes poison and grows so thick it kills all forms of vegetation around it. The Upas tree's very existence results in sheltering, shading, poisoning, and destroying its surroundings.

Unfortunately, there are people who possess the same qualities and lifestyle. They dominate, criticize, and overwhelm others while wanting attention, credit, and homage paid to them. These people have no interest in sharing themselves. They simply have not learned to love or be loved.

Several years ago a story appeared in *The Gospel Banner* that provided a clear example of an "upas person":

> A fashionably dressed young woman, sightseeing in a New York City slum, shuddered over a dirty, unkempt ragamuffin playing in the filth of the gutter. "Just look at that child!" she cried. "Why doesn't someone clean him up? Where is his mother?"
>
> "Well, it's this way, Miss," explained her tour guide. "The child's mother loves her child, but she doesn't hate the dirt. You hate the dirt, but you don't love the child. Until love for the child and hate for the dirt get into the same heart, the poor child remains just about as he is."[11]

People who have received "the blessing" will live lives full of the fruit of the Spirit and will see people through the eyes of the Spirit. Daily they will commit themselves to being servants of God and servants to the body of Christ—never demanding, never requiring, but always desirous of giving of themselves as a conduit of the Holy Spirit.

At times I hear of a Christian who is habitually treating people harshly, taking advantage of them, or behaving in unethical ways—or clearly living in a way that the Bible warns against, such as cheating, stealing, or committing adultery. There is no question that God can help these people and forgive them for what they have done; however, there is no way that they are full of the Spirit of God. Whether they have been Pentecostal or charismatic for years, or they are a preacher or someone who has been greatly used of God, they are no longer full of God's Spirit if they are habitually behaving in these ways.

The biblical lifestyle we display when we are full of the Holy Spirit is the "fruit" of the Spirit. If a person claims numerous charismatic gifts, those gifts should be accompanied by the fruit of God's Spirit. The Giver of the gifts is also the One who enables us to produce His fruit in the way we live. If a Christian does not demonstrate a life that is more effective and fulfilling than the lives of non-Christians, then unbelievers will not see Christianity as being any different than any other religion. People must see the Holy Spirit working in their lives and see that we have a living, dynamic relationship with Jesus Christ.

George Barna and his research group noted some interesting, and alarming, statistics. He said that what makes the level of biblical ignorance especially disheartening is that often there is little or no distinction between the proportion of Christians and non-Christians who know what the Bible teaches. Consider these comparisons of the born-again and non-Christian segments:

- Eighty-one percent of non-Christians believe the notion that God helps those who help themselves is taught in the Bible (compared with 80 percent of born-again Christians).

- Forty-five percent said that Jesus did not come back to physical life, but was a great teacher (compared with 30 percent of believers).

- Thirty-seven percent noted that there are some sins that not even God can forgive (compared with 29 percent of Christians).

- Sixty-eight percent of the non-Christian adults surveyed said that Satan is merely a symbol of evil (compared with 49 percent of Christians).

The statements that described the distinctiveness of Jesus Christ and the Christian faith generated the most disparate views between Christians and non-Christians. The non-Christians were far less likely to relate Christ or the Christian faith to spiritual perfection. For instance, nonbelievers were nearly twice as likely as believers to contend that Jesus committed sins (51 percent as compared with 29 percent, respectively), and were only half as likely to maintain that the Bible is totally accurate in all of its teachings (43 percent as compared with 82 percent, respectively).[12]

In another account, Barna reported that:

- Twenty-seven percent of born-again Christians have been divorced; 23 percent of non-Christians have been divorced.

- Twenty-three percent of all born-again Christians buy a lottery ticket in a typical week.

- Twenty-four percent of the born-again population believes that lying is sometimes necessary.

- Sixty-one percent of the non-Christian population say that the Holy Spirit is not real, but just a symbol of God's presence or power; 55 percent of born-again believers hold this view.[13]

The alarming point that Barna's information makes is that the statistics show relatively little difference in the beliefs and lifestyles of the American Christian and the nonreligious person. Our Christian faith ought to merge with our lifestyle outside the walls of the church. Only when nonbelievers see that our beliefs affect our personal walk will they take notice.

In their book *Keeping Your Ethical Edge Sharp*, Doug Sherman and William Hendricks cite a Gallup poll showing that 37 percent of people who attend church admit to pilfering work supplies, compared with 43 percent of those who do not attend church. Thirteen percent of the churchgoers use the company phone for long-distance personal calls, compared with 17 percent of those who do not attend.[14]

It is tragic that the statistics of the Barna and Gallup surveys indicate to us that in many issues of belief and in behavior there is little difference between the ethical opinions and practices of religious and nonreligious persons. Sherman and Hendricks say:

> The ethical conduct of Christians varies only slightly from that of non-Christians. Christians are nearly as likely as unbelievers to cheat on their income tax form, copy from other students on tests, pay money under the table to building contractors, disregard legal specifications during construction, copy a computer program without paying for it, make unreported calls on the company telephone, misrepresent a product to make a sale, and obey only the laws that are convenient for them.[15]

And missions executive Ted Engstrom comments, "The struggle of men against moral indiscretion is as old as Cain and as new as tomorrow morning's newspaper. I have worked with men of many cultures around the world, and their struggles are the same to question God, to stray from commitment to their wives and children, to love money, to seek power, to vie for position, and to quit short of their goals."[16]

Sadly, these kinds of behavior demonstrate the condition of much of the American church today. However, those who are full of the Spirit are convinced of the physical resurrection of Jesus Christ. They know that Jesus was tempted but never sinned. They are sure that God forgives all sins except blasphemy of the Holy Spirit, and they knew there is an evil kingdom in this world full of demons who are lead by a real being called Satan. These Spirit-filled believers are also full of the power of God, and his characteristics are evident in their lives. They are convinced of these things because, as Jesus promised, "the Counselor, the Holy Spirit, whom the Father will send in my name, will teach you all things and will remind you of everything I have said to you" (John 14:26).

Paul described the fruit of the Spirit in a very similar way to the way he defined love to the Corinthians. He said, "The fruit of the Spirit is love, joy, peace, patience, kindness, goodness, faithfulness, gentleness and self-control" (Gal. 5:22–53).

Those who "walk" in the Holy Spirit will exhibit these characteristics in their lives. It is no mistake that the Scriptures call the third person of the Trinity the *Holy Spirit*. One of the primary desires of the Holy Spirit is to enable us to be holy. David Lim writes in his book *Spiritual Gifts*, "The fruit develops the character and sensitivities of the believer to be used by God to meet the real needs of others. Fruit in Galatians 5:22–23 refers not just to a personal, internal state of contentment, but to a manifestation of Christlikeness by which others will be drawn to God.... Fruit reflects who we are."[17] It should be the hunger and goal of every Christian to demonstrate the fruit of the Holy Spirit. Whereas Christians are given different gifts of the Spirit, all Christians should be known for the fruit. It is a mockery when people say they are full of the Holy Spirit and do not manifest His characteristics. Every one of us needs God's help to produce His fruit, but no Christian should doubt that God will help him or her. All born-again believers have the Holy Spirit's help as they seek to change and become like Christ.

LOVE

The Greek word that refers to Christian love is *agape*. It is a giving kind of love that is concerned with seeking the highest good for people without any ulterior motives for personal gain. Many misunderstand the real meaning of love. If we define love by what we see on our television sets or the opinions of our secular society, we will not comprehend the kind of love of which Paul is speaking. Love is much more than an emotional feeling; it is a decision to do the right thing for others no matter what you feel like doing.

William Barclay has written:

> In Greek there are four words for love. (1) *Eros* means the love of a man for a maid; it is the love which has passion in it. It is never used in the New Testament at all. (2) *Philia* is the warm love which we feel for our nearest and dearest; it is a thing of the heart. (3) *Storge* rather means affection and is specially used of the love of parents and children. (4) *Agape*, the Christian word, means unconquerable benevolence. It means that no matter what a man may do to us by way of insult or injury or humiliation we will never seek anything else but his highest good. It is therefore a feeling of the mind as much as of the heart; it concerns the will as much as the emotions. It describes the deliberate effort—which we can make only with the help of God—never to seek anything but the best even for those who seek the worst of us.[18]

Bishop Stephen Neill writes that love is "a steady direction of the will toward another's lasting good."[19] He says that much so-called love is really selfish, only wanting something for itself. Agape love, however, seeks the well-being of the other person. Neill continues:

> The first love (our human love) says, "I wish to make my own something that another has, and which it is in his power to give me."
> The second love (God's love within us) says, "I wish to give to this other, because I love him."
> The first love wishes to make itself richer by receiving a gift which some other can give.
> The second love wishes to make another richer by giving all it has.
> The first love is a matter of feeling and desire. This love comes and goes as it will; we cannot call it into being by any effort of our own.
> The second love is much more a matter of the will, since to give or not to give is largely within our power.[20]

JOY

Joy has its foundation in knowing God. It is a deep appreciation for the love, grace, blessings, promises, and nearness of God that are a part of those who belong to Christ. It has little to do with what we own, how we feel, or how people have treated us. It is a deep sense of satisfaction that comes into our lives when we personally know our Creator and understand that we are His children.

I have had the opportunity to visit the location in Rome where many think the apostle Paul spent his last days. The place is a hollowed out rock below ground level. It is damp, dark, and most certainly would encourage claustrophobic feelings. In such a place he awaited the carrying out of his sentence of being beheaded, yet in spite of his circumstances, Paul had joy. He knew his eternal destiny. He knew that at the moment of death he would instantly be with the Lord. Very possibly he wrote Timothy, his dear son and friend in the faith, from death row. His writings reveal no hint of sorrow over his physical condition or death sentence. On the contrary, he instructs his readers to rejoice in the Lord always. (See Philippians 4:4.)

Charles Allen said, "Just as all the water in the world cannot quench the fire of the Holy Spirit, neither can all the troubles and tragedies of the world overwhelm the joy which the Spirit brings into the human heart."[21]

PEACE

Peace is the quietness of our emotions and our thinking that is based on the knowledge that all is well between us and our heavenly Father. Barclay said peace is "that tranquility of heart which derives from the all-pervading consciousness that our times are in the hands of God."[22] Throughout the history of the church, Christians, when going through situations that would naturally agitate or crush the average person, have had a unique ability to have "peace...which transcends all understanding" (Phil. 4:7). This peace is very different from the peace those without Christ understand. It is available to those who trust Christ and walk in the Spirit. As Charles Spurgeon said, "I looked at Christ, and the dove of peace flew into my heart; I looked at the dove of peace, and it flew away."[23] This peace is supernatural, it comes from the Holy Spirit.

PATIENCE

Three words are used in the New Testament for patience: *makrothumia, hupomone,* and *anoche. Hupomone* means persevering or bearing up under suffering or despair. *Anoche* refers to the forbearance (holding back) of God concerning humankind's sinning. The word used by Paul in Galatians 5:22 is *makrothumia*, which pertains to a great capability to be patient with people who repeatedly wrong us. Christians are to control their tempers and seek to understand others. It is one thing to try to be patient with day-to-day activities and relationships, but how do you react to people when they treat you wrongly or say things that injure your reputation? This word means endurance, being slow to anger or despair. If God were a man, he would have wiped out this world long ago; but He has patience that bears with all of our sinning, and He will not cast us off.[24] God is patient with all of humankind, not wanting anyone to be eternally lost. We are to demonstrate the same kind of patience with those who are part of our life.

KINDNESS

Kindness wants to reconcile and redeem. The word *chrestotes* is at times translated "goodness." The word stands for a goodness that is kind.[25] It does not avoid confronting someone who is wrong, nor does it overlook circumstances that could require repentance. This kindness operates in a gentle spirit. Although it does not want to hurt others or cause pain, it wants the greatest long-term good for others. Those who are kind want what Christ wants for people, knowing that if people are living sinful lives, they will ultimately bring harm to themselves. In dealing with such people, however, the kind person remembers God's mercy. Charles Allen has said, "In one's disdain of sin, one can be harsh and unkind toward a sinner....Some people seem to have such a passion for righteousness that they have no room left for compassion for those who have failed."[26] Kindness looks for others' eternal good and seeks ways to help them do what is pleasing to God.

GOODNESS

Goodness is "virtue equipped at every point."[27] Goodness (Greek *agathosune*) has a zeal for the truth and a hatred for evil; it can be expressed in acts of kindness or in rebuking and correcting evil. Its desire when rebuking or correcting is to bring out the truth and ultimate good in a person or situation. Trench says that Jesus showed *agathosune* when he cleansed the temple and drove out those who were making it a bazaar.[28] Billy Graham said, "The word *good* in the language of the Scripture literally means *to be like God,* because He alone is the One who is perfectly good.... The meaning here is more than *doing good.* Goodness goes far deeper. Goodness is love in action. It carries with it not only the idea of righteousness imputed, but righteousness in everyday living by the Holy Spirit."[29]

FAITHFULNESS

Faithfulness is a firm and unswerving loyalty and adherence to a person to whom one is united by promise, commitment, trustworthiness, and honesty.[30] Persons who are faithful are loyal and reliable to both the truth and to the people they serve. We allow God the Holy Spirit to speak to us about the areas of our lives that need to be more Christlike, such as our attitudes, thinking, and behavior. When we become aware that the Holy Spirit is making us sensitive to an area in our life that needs to be corrected and forgiven, we are quick to respond to His prompting. We are faithful to Christ and faithful to the Holy Spirit's inner voice.

GENTLENESS

Gentleness (Greek *praotes*) can also be translated "meekness." It is restraint coupled with strength and courage. It describes a person who can be angry when anger is needed and humbly submissive when submission is needed.[31] Some have accurately described it as "power under control." Aristotle defined *praotes* as the mean between excessive anger and excessive angerlessness, the quality of the person who is always angry at the right time and never at the wrong time.[32] The Holy Spirit will help us control our emotions so that we do not sin in our conversations or actions. We might feel like losing control, but God will enable us to hold steady.

In his description of South African churchman and devotional writer Andrew Murray, Wheaton College president V. R. Edman said:

> Such indeed is the abiding life that draws its sustenance and strength from the Vine. By the refreshing and reviving flow of the Holy Spirit through that life there is prayer that prevails, preaching that is powerful, love that is contagious, joy that overflows, and peace that passes understanding. It is the adoration that is stillness to know God for oneself. It is the obedience that does the Savior's bidding in the light of the Word. It is the fruitfulness that arises spontaneously from abiding in the Vine.[33]

SELF-CONTROL

Also translated as "temperance," *egkrateia* is the Greek word for self-control. It means having control or authority over one's desires and passions. Susanna Wesley once wrote to her son John, when he was studying at Oxford, "Anything which increases the authority of the body over the mind is an evil thing."[34] People who use self-control have command over their natural desires for pleasure. They are not controlled by their spontaneous impulses for earthly desires. Plato used the word *temperance* (self-control) for self-mastery.[35]

Egkrateia is the word used for athletes' discipline of their bodies. (See 1 Corinthians 9:25.) It is also the word for Christians' control of their sexuality. (1 Corinthians 7:9.) Persons who use self-control, with the help of the Holy Spirit, are masters of their emotions and impulses. They are not constantly changing their behavior or opinions with the next person's advice, but are able to hold on to what is right and true. Secular Greek uses this word as the virtue of an emperor who never lets his private interests influence the government of his people.[36]

NO LIMITS TO FRUIT

After listing the fruit of the Spirit, Paul tells us, "Against such things there is no law" (Gal. 5:23), indicating that there are no limits or restrictions over this kind of lifestyle. Christians are to literally live in and be known for these character traits. When people look at them, all of the fruit should be obvious. In his book *The Fruit of the Spirit*, Manford George Gutzke likens the fruit of the Spirit to light, "All the colors of the rainbow are in every beam of sunlight. They all are there at any one time. They may not always come into vision, but they are all present. It is not necessary to think of them as being so many separate colors. Just as these colors of the rainbow are present in light, so these traits of personal conduct are in the working of the Holy Spirit."[37]

We should pray often that our lives will be as exemplary as the lives of the Christians we read about in the New Testament. It is possible, for God has given us the Holy Spirit to help us exhibit the fruit of the Spirit in our lives. There is no negative behavior or habit that we cannot overcome with the help of the Holy Spirit. J. B. Phillips writes, "The great difference between present-day Christianity and that of which we read in these [New Testament] letters is that to us it is primarily a performance, to them it was a real experience.... To these men it is quite plainly the invasion of their lives by a new quality of life altogether. They do no hesitate to describe this as Christ 'living in' them."[38]

We cannot bear the fruit of the Spirit on our own. Everyone has tremendous ability to overcome bad habits or to begin new, good habits. However, there is much in life that we want to do or problems we want to overcome that we simply cannot in our own strength. We need the Holy Spirit's help. When the Holy Spirit fills us, He will enable us to walk in and demonstrate the fruit of the Spirit. Anglican bishop Jeremy Taylor said, "It is impossible for that man to despair who remembers that his Helper is omnipotent."[39]

In this day of millions of people claiming to be full of the Holy Spirit, we should see more Christlike demonstrations than at any time in history. Our Spirit-filled lives should point people to Jesus. When others spend time with us and watch how we live, they should have the same reaction the Sanhedrin had to Peter and John, "When they saw the courage of Peter and John and realized that they were unschooled, ordinary men, they were astonished and they took note that these men had been with Jesus" (Acts 4:13).

Chapter 5

THE SIGNS:
SIGNS AND WONDERS

THE SHORT, UNASSUMING African named Charles Makawa listened intently as his Bible school instructor[1] explained that in Jesus' ministry everything he accomplished on earth was through the power of the Holy Spirit, and that that same power is available to Spirit-filled believers today. Charles was amazed. He thought, *Could this be true? If it is true, I need to do as Jesus did.*

Charles went to a Muslim village called Naisi (*nah-EE-see*), Malawi (East Africa), to begin a new church. The hearts of the people there were hard, and it was difficult to persuade them to believe in Jesus Christ. Discouragement was a constant companion, and Charles became desperate for answers about how to reach this Muslim community for God. He asked the Lord to show him how to unlock the hardened hearts of the people in the village with major physical problems. There was a blind woman who was about thirty years old and a man who could not speak. Charles remembered the lesson from Bible School about how the same power of the Holy Spirit that Jesus had was also available to him. He asked the Lord to use him to pray for the healing of the two individuals. He knew that if they were healed, he would have the attention of the entire village.

Charles talked with the young woman and the mute man and asked them if they would permit him to pray for them. Both the woman and man were without hope and had nowhere else to turn. The woman had been blind since birth, and the man had lost his ability to speak many years earlier. They agreed on a time for Charles to pray for them and ask God for their physical healing. Charles knew what the consequences would be if his prayer did not work—the villagers' hearts would become even harder to reach.

Charles gently placed his hands on the Malawan woman and said, "In the name of Jesus, I pray that you would receive your sight." After a few moments, she lifted her eyelids expecting to see darkness, but suddenly she could see! For the first time in her life, she could see her family, the friends who cared for her, and this little man who was full of faith.

Charles then turned to the mute man and prayed, "In the name of Jesus, I pray that you will be able to speak." The man was instructed, "Say something, anything you can think of." The man sensed that a sound would come out of his mouth if he tried. He began to make a noise in his throat then formed a word with his lips and tongue. He was instantly healed, too!

Word of the healings quickly spread through the village, "The blind woman was healed when the Christian pastor prayed! The man who could not speak can now speak!"

The miracles got the attention of everyone. Now the short, quiet pastor could not build primitive shelters fast enough to hold the people who wanted to hear what he had to say. That small man quickly became a mighty spiritual giant to the people of Naisi.

Recently missionary Dean Galyen told of how he spoke in the Naisi village approximately one month after the healings. He found Pastor Makawa laying the foundation for the third church building. Dean was astonished with this new church. For several hours each day people gathered in the small, unfinished buildings praying to a God who answers prayer and performs miracles.

Dean set up his generator so he could connect a public address system and lights for the crusade service he would have that night. When evening came, many hungry seekers arrived to hear what the American missionary had to say.

During the time of singing, Dean stood next to the formerly mute man and listened as he sang the words to the Christian songs with all his heart. When it was Dean's turn, he went to the microphone and asked the young woman if she would tell the people what had happened to her. She quietly came to the front of the crowd, carefully stepping over the cords and moving around people and obstacles that were in her way. From deep within her she cried out to the people of her village, "I can tell you that, as you well know, I was blind! I could see nothing! But now I see!"

Today in the once-Muslim village there is a vibrant, growing church pastured by Charles Makawa. The people of the village are quickly turning to a living relationship with Jesus Christ and to an active faith in a God who constantly answers prayer. There is no question that these two "signs and wonders" of healing got the attention of the people of Naisi.

WHY SIGNS AND WONDERS?

One of the primary purposes of signs and wonders is evangelism. Author David Lim writes:

> Church growth scholars have pointed again and again to the Pentecostal-charismatic movement as the most powerful force in Christianity today. In spite of the movement's flaws, signs and wonders are a key to church growth around the world. Gifts are not meant to be contained within the walls of a church building. There we learn. Then we go forth and minister to others. The gifts themselves have a built-in go structure.[2]

The most consistent response from inquisitive unbelievers when they see God work in signs and wonders is amazement. They may become so convinced about the reality of God that they become Christians. God uses signs and wonders to further His purposes in advancing His kingdom. Evangelism is certainly the primary purpose for signs and wonders.

Signs and wonders also glorify God. In his book *Acts Today: Signs and Wonders of the Holy Spirit,* Ralph Harris writes, "Miracles bring glory to God by proving His existence. Miracles cause people to revere God. The power that comes with the baptism in the Holy Spirit is given not just to perform miracles but to glorify Christ."[3] This fact should remind persons used of God to give all glory and praise to Him. It is very troubling to see or hear of persons who try to bring credit to themselves because of their God-given gifts, or because He has chosen to use them. We must remind ourselves that we are only vessels the wonderful Holy Spirit uses. No matter how God chooses to use us, what we do must always bring glory to Him.

Furthermore, signs and wonders remind believers that God is active in the world today; thus, their experiences greatly increase their faith. The nature of God is miraculous. Signs and wonders are to be a natural experience when our supernatural God is present. Our God is a God who spoke this world into existence, and He has chosen to supercede His created natural laws countless times throughout history. It is God who chooses to use miracles, healings, deliverances, and other mighty works in His church. This is not a human idea, and is not natural; it is supernatural, and the creator God has chosen to exercise this means to manifest His glory.

When we read of the miracles in the Book of Acts, we should be able to say, "God can do them just the same way today." When we examine the ordinary disciples—not just the apostles—who were greatly used of God, we should be able to say, "God can use me in the same way."

Philip and Stephen were common "table waiters" in the early church. The apostles needed extra manpower to assure that necessary duties such as ministering to widows were carried out. The leaders looked for seven men who were full of the Holy Spirit and selected them to do some of the menial tasks. These seven men were willing to do whatever needed to be done, so their first ministry assignment was to "wait on tables" (Acts 6:2). These men were also known, however, for being greatly used of God. Philip and Stephen are two such examples.

We read of Philip, "When the crowds heard Philip and saw the miraculous signs he did, they all paid close attention to what he said. With shrieks, evil spirits came out of many, and many paralytics and cripples were healed. So there was great joy in that city" (Acts 8:6–8). And Scripture says of Stephen that he was "a man full of God's grace and power, [who] did great wonders and miraculous signs among the people" (Acts 6:8). If God could use two laymen like Philip and Stephen, who were willing to do whatever needed to be done, He can use us too.

THE EARLY CHURCH

The first-century church anticipated that God would demonstrate His presence with signs, wonders, and miracles when they gathered together. The supernatural was something they expected. They saw or heard about it in Jesus' ministry, and they expected it when they began going to those who had not heard about Christ. Peter said to the soon-to-be Spirit-filled believers at Cornelius's house, "You know what has happened throughout Judea, beginning in Galilee after the baptism that John preached—how God anointed Jesus of Nazareth with the Holy Spirit and power, and how he went around doing good and healing all who were under the power of the devil, because God was with him" (Acts 10:37–38).

Jesus tied the Great Commission (spreading the gospel to all the world) into the fact that signs and wonders would accompany the sharing of the gospel by first-century Christians.

He said to them, "Go into all the world and preach the good news to all creation. Whoever believes and is baptized will be saved, but whoever does not believe will be condemned. And these signs will accompany those who believe: In my name they will drive out demons; they will speak in new tongues; they will pick up snakes with their hands; and when they drink deadly poison, it will not hurt them at all; they will place their hands on sick people, and they will get well."

—Mark 16:15–18

In response to Jesus' command, the new church did all that He asked them to do. "Signs" (Greek *semeton*) that accompany Christians as they preach and teach the Bible's truths validate that what they are saying is genuine, that the kingdom of God has come to this earth in power, and that the living Jesus is active in their lives. As a result, we see signs and wonders and evangelism working together throughout the Book of Acts. Here are some of the examples:

Signs and Wonders	Evangelism/Church Growth
Acts 2:1–4	Acts 2:41–43
People were filled with the Holy Spirit and spoke in tongues.	About three thousand were added to their number
Acts 3:1–8	Acts 3:10; 4:3–4
Crippled man was healed.	"They were filled with wonder"; "Many who heard…believed."
Acts 5:1–13	Acts 5:14–15
Ananias and Sapphira lied to the Holy Spirit and died as a result.	"More and more….believed."

Acts 6:1–8	Acts 6:7
"Stephen…did great wonders and miraculous signs."	"The number of disciples…increased rapidly."
Acts 8:6–7	**Acts 8:12**
"Stephen…did great wonders and miraculous signs."	"The number of disciples…increased rapidly."
Acts 9:17	**Acts 9:31**
Saul was healed and filled with the Holy Spirit.	"The church…grew in numbers."
Acts 9:32–34	**Acts 9:35**
Paralytic was healed.	"Many people believed."
Acts 11:15	**Acts 11:21**
"The Holy Spirit came on them as…at the beginning."	"A great number…believed."
Acts 12:20–23	**Acts 11:21**
Herod was struck down (was eaten by worms and died).	"Word of God continued to increase and spread."
Acts 13:8–11	**Acts 13:12**
Elymas the sorcerer was made blind.	"When the proconsul saw…he believed."
Acts 14:3	**Acts 14:21–23**
Paul and Barnabas were enabled to do "miraculous signs and wonders."	"Won a large number."
Acts 16:25–26	**Acts 16:31–34**
Prison was opened by earthquake for Paul and Silas.	Jailer and family believed.
Acts 19:11	**Acts 19:20**
"God did extraordinary miracles through Paul."	"The word of the Lord spread."

Every one of the signs mentioned in Mark 16:17–18, except drinking poison, is mentioned in Luke's record of the happenings of the early church.[4]

- Speaking in tongues: Acts 2:4; 10:16; 19:6; see also 1 Corinthians 12:10, 30; 14:2, 5–6, 13–14, 18, 22, 27, 39

- Setting the demon-possessed free: Acts 5:15–16; 16:18; 19:11–12

- Escaping death by accidental snakebite: Acts 28:3–5

- Healing the sick: Acts 3:1–7; 8:7; 9:33–34; 14:8–10; 28:7–9

Signs and wonders are part of God's plan for reaching the world for Christ. Nowhere does Scripture suggest that signs were restricted to the first-century church. The same spiritual gifts we read about in the New Testament can be part of our lives today. Paul said to the Corinthian church, "You do not lack any spiritual gift as you eagerly wait for our Lord Jesus Christ to be revealed" (1 Cor. 1:7). There is no question that preaching the gospel of the kingdom and "bringing in the kingdom" by the demonstration of God's power through signs and wonders catches the attention of unbelievers and builds the faith of believers.[5]

Many have heard of David Yonggi Cho, the pastor of Yoido Full Gospel Church in Seoul, Korea. From an initial membership of five people in 1958, the church grew to two thousand members within five years. In his book *Fire from Heaven*, Harvey Cox explains that:

Each [member] became a dedicated messenger and recruiter, bringing others into the ever-enlarging fold. By 1971 there were 15,000 members; by 1981 there

were 200,000. The congregation now lists over 800,000*
most of whom take part in small face-to-face prayer and
study groups in addition to the plenary gatherings in the
church's massive temple. The Yoido Full Gospel Church
is still growing and its enthusiastic members insist they
will top a million by the year 2000. They probably will.[6]

Although many have heard of this amazing church, most
might not know of the powerful miracle that happened in
Cho's life that brought him to a saving faith in Jesus Christ.
Cho writes:

> My family lived in North Korea. When the war broke
> out, we lost our home. With other refugees, we traveled
> south to Pusan. Money and food were extremely scarce,
> and I worked very hard to eke out an existence of one
> meal a day and to continue my education.
>
> One day while I was working, blood came up and
> filled my mouth. Soon it was coming from my nose
> also, and I struggled to keep from choking until I lapsed
> into unconsciousness. When I came to, my clothing was
> soaked in blood. I was too dizzy to rise. How long I lay
> there, I don't know.
>
> Finally I struggled to my feet and managed to reach
> home. All night I was in and out of a coma; my fever
> rose, and when I coughed, blood gushed out.
>
> By morning I was more dead than alive. My parents
> took me to a hospital and had a doctor examine me.
> He made X-rays of my chest. Then he said, "I am very
> sorry, but we can do nothing for you. You have less than
> a month to live."
>
> "Doctor," I cried, "are you telling me the truth?"
>
> He showed me the X-rays and explained, "Your right
> lung is completely destroyed by tuberculosis. The upper
> part has collapsed, and gangrene has set in. Your left

*Church growth statisticians offer various numbers for Yoido Full Gospel
Church, usually estimating between 700,000 and 800,000 people.

lung is also tubercular. Malnutrition and hard work have caused your heart to enlarge, and it cannot circulate the blood properly. There is no medical help for these things, so I have no choice but to tell you the truth."

I returned home dazed. My father tried to reassure me. "My son, there is no life and no death, no joy and no sorrow—only in Buddha is there reality. Forget about life and death and have peace."

I protested, "The blood that I am vomiting is real; my suffering is real. Buddha and your philosophies have not helped me. I reject them all."

One day as I lay there, fear and desperation overcame me and I cried out, "Is there any God? If there is anyone called God anywhere in the universe, please come and help me! I want to make ready to die."

God heard my prayer and He answered, but in a form I least expected! A young girl knocked at my door and entered carrying a Bible. I was stunned, for in our culture women are not forward, and men dislike being taught by them. Arrogantly I ordered the girl to leave, but she said, "I can see that you are dying. I want to tell you about Christ Jesus, my Savior."

I became more angry and cursed her. I told her that millions of tuberculosis germs were flying around in the air and that she would become infected. She only replied, "My Christ will protect me," and continued to witness to me. Finally she left, and I said, "Bless Buddha, she is gone!"

The following morning she was back again. This time she sang some songs and read aloud from her Bible. I cursed and called her a Christian dog, but she did nothing against me. All day she talked of Christ.

On the fifth day when she came, I asked why she continued to come and pray for me. "There is Someone who constrains me to come here and pray for you," she replied.

"Who is it?" I asked.

She gave me her Bible, and I began reading at the place she indicated—the first chapter of Matthew. After a few minutes I exclaimed, "This is like a telephone directory. How can this help me?"

She told me to read on and I would find a wonderful story. After praying again, she left.

I read on, expecting to find difficult philosophy such as I had studied in Buddhism. But I found the Bible was about a man called Jesus Christ, the Son of God!

I read about Jesus healing the sick and dying. If only I could come to this Jesus, I thought. He would help me! Reason argued that I could not come. I had cursed and hated Him. I tried to find a Scripture verse showing that Christ hated sinners, but search as I would, I could not find one. Instead I found that He forgave an adulteress and delivered a demon-possessed man. Always He received the sick and sinful. Slowly realization came that although I was poorest of the poor, a great sinner, and dying with tuberculosis, Jesus Christ would receive me!

I decided to pray and ask Jesus to become my savior. As I prayed, a great peace showered down upon me. Every cell in my body seemed charged with new life. Something began to bubble up inside, and I thought I was going to vomit blood, but I found it was joy! I wanted to sing but I didn't know how.

After going through a lifetime of rejection from my family because I had left the Buddhist faith, I rented a small room to live in. One day, I locked the door of my room and began to pray. "Jesus," I said, "I want to meet You and have a consultation about my future." I waited, but Christ did not come. Then I shut my eyes very tightly hoping He might come in a vision. But no vision appeared. I prayed all day. By night I was soaked in perspiration, but I still prayed. After midnight the strength had left my body, and I lay down to rest.

Suddenly the room became bright. Billows of what I thought to be smoke rolled in. I was awestruck. Thinking the house was on fire, I tried to call for help, but no sound came.

In desperation I looked about and beside me I saw two feet. I looked up higher and saw a white robe. Then I looked into a face that was like a powerful sun and rays of light going outward. Still I did not know who He was until I saw the crown of thorns. They were piercing His temples and the blood was streaming down. I knew then that He was Jesus Christ. His love seemed to pour over me.

My gods had been gods of fear and curses. Always I had gone into their temples to beg them not to punish me. But Jesus was different. I felt His love, and all fear left me.

Glorious joy came from my inner being. My tongue and lips began to speak. I tried to stop, but it seemed that another person was controlling them and forcefully expressing Himself. I did not know what it was, but I realized that the more I spoke the better I felt, so I spoke and spoke.

When I became aware of my surroundings again, Jesus had gone, but the glory was still in my soul. I forgot about the pain in my heart and lungs and ran to a nearby house where a missionary I had met stayed. I knew Louis Richards, the Assemblies of God missionary, would be able to answer my questions about this experience. I explained to him that I spoke in a strange language. He opened his Bible to the second chapter of Acts and explained that I had been baptized with the Spirit as the early believers were. We cried for joy.

This new experience made me want to witness more. I went out on the streets and told people about Jesus. As I grew stronger, I went from house to house.

One day I realized that I was no longer suffering from heart pain or short breath. I went to the hospital, and after examination and X-rays the doctor told me that my lungs were well. No tuberculosis! Even my heart was its normal size.[7]

Today the Yoido Full Gospel Church in Seoul, South Korea, is the largest church in the world and in history. David Yonggi Cho is a healthy, driven man. He remembers his empty past without Christ and understands the powerless religion of his nation. Cho has experienced the miraculous power of God, and he is committed to bringing the kingdom of God to Korea with power and authority. To Pastor Cho, church growth is not in beautiful buildings or great programs (even though these may be good); rather, church growth happens naturally when people experience the mighty power of God.

Consider the story of Peter and John going to the temple to pray in Acts 3:1–10. A crippled man was brought to the temple gate every day where he begged for money. He had been born crippled and had no hope of walking, so someone had to carry him to his begging spot. He sat on the dusty ground and looked up at the people walking by and cried out for a little money.

If you live in a large city, this is not an uncommon sight. All of us have seen beggars. Sometimes we feel guilty because we cannot help them. At times we become angry because they bother us or we do not like seeing them. Perhaps sometimes we wish they were healed.

When Peter and John walked past the beggar, the beggar thought they were just two ordinary men. He probably did not pay particular attention to anyone walking by. The crowd was just a blur of people. Many years before, his emotions had grown numb with defeated acceptance that this was his lot in life. Looking toward the people, he may have cried out in an echoing monotone, "Alms, alms, alms. Do you have any alms?" We have heard this before. "Can you spare any change?" Or it could have sounded like, "I need money to feed my family."

Peter may have walked by this man before. In fact, he probably had walked by a lot of beggars in his lifetime. But this day, he felt a faith surge up inside him, and he stopped walking to look at the man. He may have taken John by the arm and said, "Stop, John! Hold it for a minute! I want to talk to this man."

> Peter looked straight at him, as did John. Then Peter said [to the man], "Look at us!" So the man gave them his attention, expecting to get something from them.
>
> Then Peter said, "Silver or gold I do not have, but what I have I give you. In the name of Jesus Christ of Nazareth, walk." Taking him by the right hand, he helped him up, and instantly the man's feet and ankles became strong. He jumped to his feet and began to walk. Then he went with them into the temple courts, walking and jumping, and praising God.
>
> —ACTS 3:4–8

Would you have not done the same? I know I would have. I would have run, jumped, laughed, and cried. I do not believe that I would have been embarrassed or cared for a moment what people thought of me. I also would have immediately wanted to hear whatever this guy named Peter had to say.

A crowd did gather around the three men, because many remembered that this was "the beggar." When Peter saw that people were staring at them, he said:

> Men of Israel, why does this surprise you? Why do you stare at us as if by our own power or godliness we had made this man walk? The God of Abraham, Isaac and Jacob, the God of our fathers, has glorified his servant Jesus. You handed him over to be killed, and you disowned him before Pilate, though he had decided to let him go. You disowned the Holy and Righteous One and asked that a murderer be released to you. You killed the author of life, but God raised him from the dead. We are witnesses of this. By faith in the name of Jesus, this man whom you see and know was made strong. It is Jesus' name and the faith that comes through him that has given this complete healing to him, as you can all see.
>
> —ACTS 3:12–16

Peter took advantage of the crowd's wonderment to explain to them that the resurrected Jesus healed the man and that they could receive forgiveness of their sins and receive salvation by believing in Jesus Christ. There is no question that when God performs a miracle, people are open to a gospel presentation.

WHY DO SOME DOUBT SIGNS AND WONDERS?

I have had the privilege of traveling to many countries where signs and wonders are a common occurrence. Testimonies of mighty acts of God are a part of many worship services in these and other countries. However, in America there has been much skepticism, criticism, and even teaching against the reality of God using powerful signs in the church of today. This is in part due to the extreme unbelief that we are constantly exposed to in the American media and press. Television programming often mocks those with faith in God or with strong religious convictions. Some radio talk show hosts use great articulate talent to create doubt about the power of God. We have a generation of people who are experts in unbelief and who boldly mock reports of God's power by saying, "Ridiculous!" Many in America believe that money and possessions, not spiritual truth, will bring ultimate happiness. If you do not believe this, just watch the commercials for one evening on your local programming.

Most of our school systems forbid our children to pray publicly. They forbid Bible studies and remove nativity scenes, Christmas cards about Christ, and Christian pictures. At the same time, they insist on the rights of homosexuals and the ability to teach that there are alternative types of sexual behavior—that is, premarital, extramarital, homosexual, and lesbian. They promote the free distribution of condoms because they assume that all young people are sexually active. They push for laws that will permit minors to take the life of their unborn child without informing their parents, yet they fight for the rights of animals.

Our society is not a Christian society as many think. It is far from God's standards and is full of the sickening apathy that comes from affluence. Americans have a lot of hang-ups that some other nations simply do not have.

In many other parts of the world, the Christian's faith is often a simple and innocent belief in an ever-present, ever-active, mighty God. Americans tend to complicate it or try to figure it out, but Jesus said that we must come to Him like children. "I tell you the truth, unless you change and become like little children, you will never enter the kingdom of heaven" (Matt. 18:3).

In spite of all the sin, I believe America is on the brink of a great revival. More and more I am hearing from desperate, hungry people and churches that are experiencing God in a fresh way and as a result are growing tremendously. Signs and wonders are becoming more common in many church settings today.

There are several reasons why people doubt miracles and signs and wonders:

1. They have never—or think they have never—experienced or witnessed signs and wonders.

There is no question that this is the biggest reason why some do not believe in the miraculous gifts of the Spirit today. In his excellent book *Surprised by the Spirit*, Jack Deere writes, "Christians do not disbelieve in the miraculous gifts of the Spirit because the Scriptures teach these gifts have passed away. Rather they disbelieve in the miraculous gifts of the Spirit because they have not experienced them." Deere relates a conversation he had with a well-known theologian, "I made the comment that there was not a shred of evidence in the Bible that the gifts of the Spirit had passed away. He said, 'I would not go that far, but I know that you cannot prove the cessation of the gifts by Scripture. However, we do not clearly see them in the later history of the church, and they are not part of our own theological tradition.'" Deere adds, "This man taught a seminary that was dogmatically cessationist[8] in its approach to miraculous gifts, but in private conversation he freely admitted that this doctrine could not be proved by Scripture."[9]

When reading the Scripture, one cannot come to the conclusion that the gifts ended with the early church. The great battle that many face is with the idea that they have not seen or experienced signs and wonders in their own lives.

2. They lack faith to believe in the signs and wonders.

It takes faith to believe that God exists, that the Bible is true, that Jesus is the Son of God born of a virgin, that Jesus was physically resurrected from the dead, and that He has personally forgiven you of your sins. It also takes faith to believe that God can give you the same experiences that the early Christians had and that you can do what they did. In fact, the Bible says, "Without faith it is impossible to please God" (Heb. 11:6). The way we build our faith is by hearing, reading, and meditating on God's Word. When we read about the people of God who were greatly used of God, we naturally hunger to be used in the same ways to do what they did.

3. They are attracted to the intellectual appeal of unbelief.

Signs and wonders are dumbfounding to the intellect because they go against the natural order and reverse the process of entropy. The mind wants to understand them, to figure them out, but since they are in the realm of the miraculous, the human intellect cannot figure them out. Finite minds cannot comprehend the ways of an infinite god. We simply have to believe—and that is tough for some people.

4. They may have seen the gifts misused.

Seeing the gifts misused may cause people to doubt or become critical of the validity of the gifts of the Spirit. Some scam artists have tried to trick people into believing they were seeing the work of God. They will oneday answer to God. Just because someone misuses, tries to manipulate, or pretends to be used with God's gifts, however, does not invalidate the reality of God using someone else. There will always be those who try to trick people for their own personal interests. The devil has counterfeited God's miraculous acts for thousands of years and is intensifying his activity in our time. We should not let this discourage our belief that miracles are for today.

DISCERNING TRUE FROM FALSE SIGNS AND WONDERS

Some poisons look very much like drinking water. If two glasses are placed on your counter, one full of a clear poison and the other full of drinking water, both may look the same. You could easily make the tragic mistake of picking up the poison and drinking it. While the glass of water would refresh you, the glass of poison would kill you. If you knew one glass was water and the other poison, you would have to discover which one was poison without tasting it, for the very taste could harm you.

This is the case with signs and wonders in the world today. There is no question that for thousands of years God has utilized signs and wonders to advance His kingdom. On the other hand, we also understand from Scripture that Satan uses his servants to perform "counterfeit miracles, signs and wonders" (2 Thess. 2:9). Both real and the unreal look much the same to the non-Christian's eye, but God gives believers discernment and ways to determine which miracles come from God and which have the poison of Satan in them.

In the Old Testament, Satan used people to perform counterfeit miracles by their "secret arts" (Exod. 7:11, 22; 8:7). In the New Testament, Jesus warned, "Many will say to me on that day, 'Lord, Lord, did we not prophesy in your name, and in your name drive out demons and perform many miracles?' Then I will tell them plainly, 'I never knew you'" (Matt. 7:22–23). Jesus also cautioned that "false Christs and false prophets will appear and perform great signs and miracles to deceive even the elect—if that were possible" (Matt. 24:24).

Paul instructed that the Antichrist will deceive people by using "counterfeit miracles" (2 Thess. 2:9) and "great and miraculous signs" (Rev. 13:13); but he finally will be stopped and captured when the Lord returns at the end of the Tribulation. John says that during this seven-year period demon spirits will be actively "performing miraculous signs" (Rev. 16:14).

We must not accept a person's "ministry" just because signs and wonders seem to be part of what they do. Discernment is more critical today than ever. There are several questions we should ask ourselves before we decide to believe and follow a person's teaching or spiritual leadership:

1. Does the person accurately teach or preach from the Bible?

The Bible is God's inerrant Word, and it will never lead us astray. If a teacher either ignores the Scripture or just throws a verse in here or there to make a point, be suspicious of the person's motive and of the results that person claims to be a part of his or her ministry.

Does this teacher/preacher "live" in the Word of God? Does he or she freely communicate love for the Bible? Refer to it contextually in his or her message? Use examples from Scripture? Endeavor to be accurate in the interpretation of the text? All of these questions are healthy to ask.

2. Does the person give the glory to God, or does he or she seem to be concerned about getting a reputation?

God is the giver of the gifts, but at times people want to honor the man or woman who is being used by God. This person should always be careful to reflect any praise or gratitude back to the Lord.

Paul and Barnabas had an experience in which a man who had never walked was suddenly healed:

> He listened to Paul as he was speaking. Paul looked directly at him, saw that he had faith to be healed and called out, "Stand up on your feet!" At that, the man jumped up and began to walk. When the crowd saw what Paul had done, they shouted in the Lycaonian language, "The gods have come down to us in human form!"
>
> But when the apostles Barnabas and Paul heard of this, they tore their clothes and rushed out into the crowd, shouting: "Men, why are you doing this? We too are only men, human like you. We are bringing you good news, telling you to turn from these worthless things to the living God, who made heaven and earth and sea and everything in them."
>
> —ACTS 14:9–11, 14–15

Paul and Barnabas were careful to give the glory to God for this healing miracle.

3. Can the miracle be verified by a doctor's report, or is the authenticity of the miracle obvious to those around the person who experienced it?

For example, is a blind person suddenly able to see, a paralyzed person able to walk, or a physically or mentally ill person quickly healed? When a person receives physical or emotional healing, there is obvious evidence that can be verified by trained professionals and people who have known the person. True physical healings, miracles, bring wonder to people because of the fact that they actually happened. God supernaturally reversed nature.

4. Is there godly fruit in the person's life, and are people coming into God's kingdom because of this person's ministry?

The person being used of God to pray for people's healing

or for a miracle should demonstrate the fruit of the Spirit. The Holy Spirit is never rude, greedy, arrogant, or manipulative. This is not to say that the person will not be bold, confident, or even aggressive with the gifts God has given him or her; however, this person will remind others of Christ in the way he or she acts and speaks. When Christian leaders model authentic biblical Christianity in their day-to-day activities, the positive impact on those who are observing is significant. The leader's private life must model and represent the Christlike life as much as his or her public life. And the sign or wonder will point people to Jesus Christ.

Another fruit of this person's ministry should be people being saved. Are people coming to God's kingdom as a result of this person's ministry?

There is no question that we need to use discernment as we evaluate whether a ministry is authentic or not. Some cunning people have realized that it is human nature to be impressed by signs and wonders and that naïve people will do almost anything to experience something supernatural. These religious scam artists take advantage of people's innocence.

Tertullian said, "What is daintier food to the spirit of evil than turning men's minds away from the true God by the illusions of a false divination?"[10] Satan has tried to counterfeit God's gifts for thousands of years, and in these last days he will intensify his efforts.

GOD CAN HELP YOU

As we end this chapter, we cannot help but think of the possibility that you need a miracle from God. If discouragement and hopeless thoughts have been your constant companions, we believe that God knows about your situation and wants to greatly encourage you. As you read Scripture you can feel assured that the God of the Bible is the God of today. He can be as active in your life as He was in the lives of the people you read about in the Bible. Our Christian life is a life of faith; however, a sign, wonder, miracle, or revelation from God could come to you unexpectedly in a unique way.

Dr. Arthur Guruswamy, a clinical microbiologist, had such an experience when he became very concerned that he could find no cure for two of his patients who had very serious infections. The doctor went through his normal routine of trying to isolate the infections so that he could treat them appropriately with medication. As he studied the cultures, they did not yield the reason for the infections. This greatly concerned the young doctor because of the very real possibility of these infections becoming a crisis and affecting thousands of lives around the world. The stark reality of the seriousness of the problem hit him one day. Dr. Guruswamy said, "No one knew the system for cultivating this organism."

Along with his tremendous medical training, Dr. Guruswamy had also been trained by Pentecostal and charismatic teachers that he could pray and ask God for a miracle or revelation when facing difficult times. He said, "One night as I was praying, the Lord gave me insight into how to do this." Later, when he fell asleep, he had a dream. In his dream he saw himself doing certain procedures that isolated the infectious organism. When he awoke he remembered the dream and quickly went to his lab to see if it would work. To his amazement the formula did work. God had given him the solution to the problem in a way that he did not expect. Both of his patients were successfully treated, and he became the first in the United States to isolate the organism. This was a significant event, because the organism is implicated in human infertility.

With amazement Dr. Guruswamy thought about how God had given him a solution that could not be found in a textbook or in his highly skilled training. It was so simple; it was so different from how most of the world thinks. The living God sovereignly intervened in two hopeless patients' lives through the Spirit-filled prayers of an unknown microbiologist, and as a result, thousands were helped because of this revelation.[11]

You can pray too. You can ask God to bring a specific solution to your problem. You can ask the Lord for a revelation, a miracle, or understanding into the reason why you are in the challenging situation you are in. We are convinced that He will help you—perhaps in a way you never expected.

Chapter 6

THE CHARISMA:
SPIRITUAL GIFTS

S IXTEEN-YEAR-OLD KAREN THOUGHT a ride home from a
wedding reception with a nineteen-year-old boy would
be relatively uneventful, but the combination of her bad
choices and being taken advantage of changed the course of
her life.

That evening at the reception Karen had experimented
with alcohol. She knew better and, in fact, had grown up in
a Christian home where alcohol use was avoided. During the
course of the evening, she sneaked drinks from the bar several
times. She liked the buzz and did not realize that her sense of
restraint was weakening. When the older teenager, and friend
of the family, offered her a ride home, she accepted. Before he
took Karen home, he took advantage of her sexually. Thus, the
evening when she took her first drink began a downward spiral of behavior that eventually included not only alcohol and
sex, but also drugs, diet pills, and bulimia. She was running
from her shame and desperately trying to find some meaning
in a life that had become miserable.

Karen thought that getting married would make her happy.
Later she would tell the story by saying, "When I was sixteen, I
met a twenty-three-year-old man who became my husband—
and my new drinking buddy." From the beginning, the marriage was dysfunctional and, at times, dangerous. Both Karen
and her husband became physically and mentally abusive when

they drank. One night her husband beat her so badly that she needed plastic surgery to repair the injuries to her face.

Karen left her husband, moved in with a drug smuggler, and became addicted to cocaine. She did not know what to do. She thought that if she moved back with her husband, she would find the stability in life for which she hungered. When she moved back, she found that he too had become involved in dealing cocaine. He was as messed up as she was. Life was an empty blur to Karen as she went from drugs to alcohol and tried to control her weight by forcing herself to vomit. Bulimia became a life-controlling habit.

After the loss of a newborn, Karen tried to end her life, thinking, "I'll just overdose on sleeping pills and everything will go away." The paramedics were called and she was rushed to the hospital emergency room where her life was saved.

Although Karen had run far from the Christian lifestyle she had experienced as a child, she still had not forgotten her spiritual roots. One Sunday she decided to attend a Pentecostal church to which a friend had invited her. When she walked into the building, she sensed that she was in a good place. Oddly, she felt at home among strangers.

Thinking back, she says, "I'll never forget the morning I went to church. People were clapping, raising their hands, and praising God. I wanted what these people had." The people she met were friendly, happy, and seemed to have a sense of purpose. Many were using their particular abilities and gifts as they invested in the lives of others. They prayed for Karen and sincerely believed that God would perform a miracle of deliverance and emotional healing.

The next Sunday she went back she decided to surrender her life to Jesus Christ. She immediately knew she had done the right thing and a sense of contentment settled in her heart. Finally, the days of running from God had ended for Karen. The residue of drugs and alcohol were still there, but she found a peace that no form of substance abuse had ever given her.

Shortly after Karen's new birth, she had an experience that overwhelmed her. During one church service, she had a vision. She says, "In my vision, the Lord was embracing me, and He said, 'Karen, all of these years I've had my arms open and waiting for you. Now that I have you, I will never let you go.'" In this vision, she knew that the Lord was assuring her of His love, but she also felt a sense of faith and a new strength to walk away from alcohol, drugs, and bulimia.

God miraculously delivered Karen from alcohol, diet pills, and her eating disorder. He did something else for Karen, too. After observing the change in Karen's life, her husband decided to give his life to Jesus as well.

Today this family is stable. The curse of abuse, drugs, and spiritual emptiness has been broken. If you met Karen and her husband, you would never know the incredible past and paralyzing addictions that were a part of their lives for years.[1]

The church that Karen and her family attend is like thousands of churches in the world where the gifts of the Holy Spirit are active. A miracle took place in Karen and her husband as they sensed the love of God extended toward them through the people of this church.

DIVERSITY OF GIFTS

In a church where the gifts of the Spirit are being taught and exercised in an orderly way, there is a sense of teamwork, a feeling that the congregation is working together for God's kingdom.

Someone has imagined the following story taking place among some animals shortly after Creation.

It wasn't too long after creation that the animals got together to form a school. They wanted the best school possible—one that offered their students a well-rounded curriculum of swimming, running, climbing, and flying. In order to graduate, all the animals had to take all the courses.

The duck was excellent at swimming. In fact, he was better than his instructor. But he made only passing grades at climbing and got a very poor grade in running. The duck was so slow in running that he had to stay after school every day to practice. Even with that, there was little improvement. His webbed feet got badly worn from running, and with such worn feet, he was the only able to get an average grade in swimming. Average was quite acceptable to everyone else, so no one worried much about it—except the duck.

The rabbit was at the top of her class in running. But after a while, she developed a twitch in her leg from all the time she spent in the water trying to improve her swimming.

The squirrel was a peak performer in climbing but was constantly frustrated in the flying class. His body became so bruised from all the hard landings that he did not do too well in climbing and ended up being pretty poor in running.

The eagle was a continued problem student. She was severely disciplined for being a nonconformist. For example, in climbing class, she would always beat everyone else to the top of the tree but insisted on using her own way to get there.

Each of the animals had a particular area of expertise. When they did what they were designed to do, they excelled. When they tried to operate outside their area of expertise, they were not nearly as effective.

Can ducks run? Sure they can. Is that what they do best? Definitely not.[2]

Every human being in God's kingdom is different. We have unique ancestries, experiences, and personalities. Every Christian also has diverse "spiritual gifts" (1 Cor. 12:1, 7). When we come together in the church, some people's natural or supernatural gifts stand out more than others. Some people are more vocal and obvious, and some quietly do their God-given duty for the King with few on this earth ever knowing their contribution. However, all work together for the glory of God and the advancement of his kingdom. Paul said:

> There are different kinds of gifts, but the same Spirit. There are different kinds of service, but the same Lord. There are different kinds of working, but the same God works all of them in all men.
>
> Now to each one the manifestation of the Spirit is given for the common good. To one there is given through the Spirit the message of wisdom, to another the message of knowledge by means of the same Spirit, to another faith by the same Spirit, to another gifts of healing by that one Spirit, to another miraculous powers, to another prophecy, to another distinguishing between spirits, to another speaking in different kinds of tongues, and to still another the interpretation of tongues. All these are the work of one and the same Spirit, and he gives them to each one, just as he determines.
>
> —1 CORINTHIANS 12:4–11

Theologian Gordon D. Fee says of the preceding passage, "Everything in this opening paragraph[3] revolves around the two ideas expressed in the opening sentence: 'There are different kinds of gifts, but the same Spirit.'"[4] To clarify his point, Fee illustrates the passage by using bold letters to emphasize diversities and italics to emphasize sameness.

VERSE 4	Diversities	of gifts	there are, *but the same spirit*
VERSE 5	Diversities	of service	there are, *but the same Lord*
VERSE 6	Diversities	of workings	there are, *but the same God* who works **all things in all people.**

VERSE 7	To each	is given the manifestation *of the Spirit for the common good.*	
VERSE 8	To one	is given a message of wisdom	*through the Spirit;*
	To another	a message of knowledge	*by the same Spirit:*
VERSE 9	To another	faith	*by the same Spirit;*
	To another	gifts of healings	*by the same Spirit;*
VERSE 10	To another	workings of miracles;	
	To another	prophecy;	
	To another	discernment of spirits;	
	To another	kinds of tongues;	
	To another	interpretation of tongues;	
VERSE 11	**All these things** work of *the one and the same Spirit*, **distributing** to **each one**, even as he wills.		

The emphasis and flow of the argument are easy to see. Diversity has its roots in God Himself. He in turn by His Spirit has given diverse manifestations (gifts) to different people for the common good of the community.[5]

The spiritual gifts are for edifying the church and enabling God's people to reach a lost world. Because of His love and care for the church God has given unique charismatic gifts that will build it up and strengthen it. God saw that supernatural gifts would be necessary for the health of the church because He is a supernatural God and we live in a world where the supernatural enemy actively tries to deceive and destroy people.

Throughout the ages, God was able to see the spiritual conflict with Satan the church would face. He was also able to see the turn of the twentieth century, when, more than at any time in history, there would be tremendous growth in the church and tremendous growth in evil throughout the world. Not only is there a revival in the church, but sadly, in society, there is an increase in mysticism, occultism, the paranormal, and counterfeit miracles.

The church of Jesus Christ is to show spiritual reality—the true, supernatural, pure, and powerful spiritual gifts—to a very spiritually naïve world.

SPIRITUAL GIFTS HELP US SERVE

Going back to this chapter's earlier illustration, what was it that convinced Karen that her life could be different? Countless times she had tried to change her life on her own. She had cried out for deliverance and had frantically sought for some kind of relief from her empty existence. It was when Karen watched people working together for God, saw people pray and believe for miracles for those who were hurting, and saw stable families that she seemed to be able to "just believe" and have more faith. When someone spoke in tongues during the worship services, someone else carefully interpreted what was said, and the people were encouraged. Some people in the church seemed to have a unique wisdom that was beyond education or experience. It was deep yet easy to understand, spiritual, practical, and right. God seemed to be alive and active in this church. The preacher was not the only one working, praying for the hurting, and ministering. God's people were acting together.

This is the way God has always intended the church to operate. Everyone has one or more spiritual gifts that they are to use when the body comes together as well as in their daily lives. In *Beyond Church Growth*, Robert E. Logan writes, "A church body is designed to function as a mutually dependent team, together discovering and fulfilling the assignment that God has given them."[6]

You have spiritual gifts that the Holy Spirit has given you. You might not know what they are at this time, but nevertheless, you have one or more. "Now to *each one* the manifestation of the Spirit is given for the common good" (1 Cor. 12:7, emphasis added).

One weakness in some Pentecostal/charismatic churches is that they have majored in only two of the gifts of the Spirit—tongues and interpretation. The Bible does not give greater priority to these two gifts. It is God's desire that all of the charismatic gifts be active. In addition to tongues and interpretation, there are the gifts of wisdom, knowledge, faith, healing, miraculous powers, prophecy, and discernment. He has created these spiritual gifts for our good and for the health of the church. All of the gifts are meant to bring comfort and encouragement to the body of Christ.

God designed, planted, and established the church, and He also wrote the "rule book" on how it is to operate most effectively. In the Bible God has instructed us to use the spiritual gifts and has given us specific directions on how to use them most effectively (1 Corinthians 12–14). Theologian Frederic Godet writes, "The term Charisma indicates rather their [the gifts'] origin, the word *pneumatika* (14:1) their essence."[7] In other words, the gifts originate with God, and their essential nature is from the Holy Spirit. The word *charisma* was not found in the Septuagint or in Greek writings before the Christian era. It occurs almost exclusively in Paul's writings (one usage being in 1 Peter). Paul considers the church and the gifts integral to each other—if this is the church, these are the gifts. If these are the gifts, they picture the church.[8]

The church is the greatest institution on earth. When the church comes together, it ought to reflect who Christ is through the work of the Spirit. It is comprised of born-again people from every Christian denomination, race, and nation. Even though there are many problems and challenges in the church, it is a beautiful organization full of God's people. God has given the church all of the gifts necessary to make it effective in a sinful and terribly lost world.

HAVE YOU DISCOVERED YOUR SPIRITUAL GIFTS?

God is looking for people He can use. A woman in a Detroit church where I used to pastor had the gift of healing. Over the years I watched as she was able to believe for physical and emotional healing in many people's lives.[9] I have a friend who has great faith for couples who, because of physical reasons, are unable to have children. Numerous times this person has prayed for couples and they have experienced a miracle resulting in pregnancy. The doctors have no explanation for them except that something changed.

Every member of the body of Christ has been given a spiritual gift or gifts, but few understand what their gifts are. In a recent random survey of at least one thousand selected adults, George Barna discovered that 72 percent say they are church members;[10] however, 29 percent of all adults—and 40 percent of baby busters—have never heard of spiritual gifts, and 69 percent have heard of spiritual gifts but do not know what their spiritual gifts are. The most common gift claimed by church-goers is the gift of teaching (5 percent). The most common items mentioned as spiritual gifts (which are not biblical gifts) are love, kindness, relationships, singing, and listening. The groups least familiar with spiritual gifts are baby busters—60 percent; seniors—61 percent; low-income adults—66 percent; and those not born-again—62 percent.[11]

These statistics remind us of the ignorance there is on the subject of spiritual gifts. We believe, however, that Christian people do want to know about the gifts God has given them and how to use them. Statistics indicate that many of the churches that encourage the use of charismatic gifts are growing.

A recent survey was taken in which church leaders were

asked, "When you changed the way you helped people find a place of service [using their spiritual gifts], was there a change in your attendance? Twenty-seven percent indicated that it caused growth–resulting in a median of twenty-five new people added in the previous year. The survey discovered that growing churches actively assist people in finding their spiritual gifts and encourage them to use the gifts that God has given them. Many of the fastest growing churches were more likely to offer classes on spiritual gifts. Forty-seven growing churches were more likely to offer classes on spiritual gifts. Forty-seven percent indicated that they hold occasional spiritual gift seminars, and another 21 percent offer ongoing classes.[12] The fastest-growing churches were more likely to offer the most active methods—an ongoing spiritual gifts class. Slower-growing or declining churches tended not to offer an ongoing class.[13]

Why are these churches growing? Because members feel that they are part of the overall program. They are not just observers; they are active participants. They feel important—and they are—because they are part of a unit that is working together for God's kingdom. Greg Ogden writes in *The New Reformation*, "The church's ministry is shaped by the gifts and callings distributed by the Holy Spirit to the whole body of Christ."[14] And Rick Warren says in *The Purpose Drive Church*:

> The greatest need in evangelical churches is the release of members for ministry. A Gallup survey discovered that only 10 percent of American church members are active in any kind of personal ministry and that 50 percent of all church members have no interest in serving in any ministry.... The encouraging news that Gallup uncovered is this: Forty percent of all members have expressed an interest in having a ministry, but they have never been asked or they don't know how. This group is an untapped gold mine! If we can mobilize this 40 percent and add them to the current 10 percent already serving,

your church could have 50 percent of its members active in a ministry.[15]

WHY SPIRITUAL GIFTS?

Uruguay is a hotbed of intense spiritual oppression and satanic worship. Approximately 50 percent of the nation's inhabitants are atheists. Thousands of witches line up on the beaches of Uruguay annually for demonic rituals. Many caring missionaries, pastors, and churches have intensely prayed for spiritual breakthrough in this needy country.

Recently, before a crusade meeting, a worker named Blanqui was praying for God to do mighty things during the services and for the Lord to remove any hindrances from those who wanted to attend. During her prayer time, something unusual happened to her. She saw a vision of a bright light in the shape of a virgin dressed in blue in the balcony of the church, which is an old theater. Later, in a prayer meeting, she told missionary Don Triplett and the other crusade leaders about the vision. They wondered what it might have meant, but they did not tell anyone else about Blanqui's experience.

Soon after this, Don was speaking to a man who had been involved in Satan worship for thirteen years but was now a Christian. Don mentioned to the man that often a demon-possessed person is the "strongman" for the devil in the villages and cities. The man then said to Don, "The strongman of this area is a statue idol of a virgin along the ocean. About a million Macomberos [Satanists] in Uruguay worship this idol."

Don told the man about the vision Blanqui had seen when she was in prayer.

"I need to talk to her to see if she saw this idol," the man quickly said.

When Blanqui described the vision to the ex-Satanist, Don got goose bumps all over and realized that the Spirit of God had revealed the exact shape, color, location, and every other detail of the idol to her. God supernaturally gave her specific insight about what to pray for.

Four days after this experience, the crusade began. An amazing thing happened. A dynamic spiritual breakthrough occurred, and approximately seven hundred people were saved, delivered from demonic spirits that possessed them, and baptized in the Holy Spirit.[16]

Some might wonder about dreams and visions that Christians sometimes experience, but Scripture tells us:

> In the last days, God says, I will pour out my Spirit on all people. Your sons and daughters will prophesy, your young men will see visions, your old men will dream dreams.
>
> —ACTS 2:17

When God gives a gift (or gifts) of the Spirit to an individual, it is not just for a personal experience; it is for service. We are to use these gifts for the benefit of others. The gifts of the Spirit enable us to work in God's kingdom and help those to whom we endeavor to witness.

God does not want us to be ignorant about spiritual gifts. (See 1 Corinthians 12:1.) He wants us to utilize them in our service to the church as well as in outward ministry to a world in which most people are without Christ. Bible commentator Arnold Bittlinger has rightly said, "The origin of a charisma never lies in the person, but in God's grace which surrounds him. It is essential to bear in mind this origin whenever the gift is considered or experienced."[17]

The nine gifts are collectively called "the manifestation of the Spirit" (1 Cor. 12:7), the demonstration or display of the Spirit in our lives. God utilizes each person's unique personality and manifests one or more of the gifts through that person. As certain athletes are naturally gifted and coordinated in running, shooting, passing, or catching a ball, so are people who manifest spiritual gifts naturally gifted. The gifts stand out, or display, themselves. As an athlete is expected to be part of the larger team and work as a "team member," so are members of the body of Christ to cooperate with the goals of God for his church. There are to be no mavericks in God's church. We are servants and fellow strugglers in God's kingdom. We work for the good of the other members and for the cause of reaching those without Christ. Pastor David Lim of Grace Assembly of God in Singapore has accurately said, "The Church is a diversity, yet must act in unity. The Church is one, yet must demonstrate its diversity."[18]

NINE CHARISMA GIFTS

Every person in the body of Christ has a purpose and a divine mandate on his or her life. No human being is a mistake; each is not only personally important to God but is critical to the overall plan God has for His church. The baptism in the Holy Spirit is available to help you be all that you can be for the glory of God. God has provided this wonderful experience to benefit you. It does not make you "more saved" or closer to heaven, but it enables you to be more effective for God's kingdom. Lim writes:

> The baptism in the Spirit is not primarily a qualifying experience but an equipping experience. It enables Christians to do the job more effectively. The person who is fully yielded to the Holy Spirit will find a greater dimension of ministry than could be realized without the infilling. But this does not negate the importance or ministry of anyone who has not yet experienced the blessing. That would defeat the principle of body ministry. Such persons, however, should be encouraged to claim the promise of the Holy Spirit. Gifts are given to every member. As we yield to the Holy Spirit, we are further empowered for service.[19]

Many have divided the nine charisma gifts of 1 Corinthians 12:8–11 into three categories. While we should not become involved in a great debate over the issue of how to divide the gifts, it is helpful to envision the gifts in this way:

TEACHING GIFTS

- Message of wisdom
- Message of knowledge

POWER MINISTRY GIFTS (WITHIN THE CHURCH AND TO THE WORLD)

- Faith
- Gifts of healing
- Miraculous powers
- Prophecy
- Distinguishing between spirits

SPEAKING GIFTS

- Speaking in different kinds of tongues
- Interpretation of tongues

People who have gifts in the teaching area may also be used in the gifts of power. People who have the gift of giving messages in tongues may also interpret or be used in the teaching or power gifts. One does not need to assume that he or she is "slotted" with a certain gift. The Holy Spirit can choose to utilize us in any gift as the need arises; however, one will notice that particular gifts seem to stand out in the ministry God has given a certain person.

MESSAGE OF WISDOM

All of the gifts are to help the body of Christ. When we have knowledge about a particular truth, something we need to do, or an issue in someone's life, God will give us the wisdom as to how and when to apply this knowledge. Wisdom and knowledge often work together. Whenever the gift of wisdom is used, it reveals God's purpose and plans and does not contradict Scripture. When the apostles were trying to find a way to care for the widows, they chose seven men who were "known to be full of the Spirit and wisdom" (Acts 6:3). They knew in advance that these men would deal wisely and be led by the Holy Spirit as they tried to find ways to help the widows.

We need wisdom in our daily lives whether leading a ministry program in our church, counseling a friend, or doing our job. The Book of Proverbs encourages us to place highest priority on seeking God's wisdom when we are making decisions. We should always ask, "What is God's will concerning this matter and how does He want me to deal with this situation?" As we grow spiritually, we become more sensitive to the Holy Spirit's wisdom in our everyday affairs and learn to seek the mind of God. The Bible encourages us, "If any of you lacks wisdom, he should ask God, who gives generously to all without finding fault, and it will be given to him" (James 1:5). It could be that you need God's insights on how to help your child. Perhaps you need divine wisdom with a difficulty in your marriage or a rift that has occurred in another relationship. Knowledge gives us the "what" information, and wisdom gives the "how to" information. God's wisdom is available to everyone in His church; however, some people seem to be known for their use of this particular gift. Typically (and hopefully) these are the men and women who are used in teaching ministries or leadership positions of the church.

MESSAGE OF KNOWLEDGE

Early Pentecostal church leader Donald Gee described messages of knowledge as "flashes of insight into truth that penetrated beyond the operation of their own unaided intellect."[20] This spiritual gift helps the teacher communicate the truths found in the Bible. Often the Sunday school teacher or Bible study leader will think of a unique way to help listeners understand what the Scripture is saying; it could be through an illustration or an example that comes to mind perhaps from another portion of the Bible. The end result is that the students "get it" and can apply it to their lives.

God has given military leaders instructions about how to fight a battle, and He gives spiritual leaders insight into how Satan fights against the church. God has also used this gift to supernaturally reveal to parents a situation in their child's life. He has told church leaders specific information about sin in the life of a troubled person with whom they must deal. Nathan "knew" about David's sin with Bathsheba, his murder of her husband, Uriah, and the resulting cover-up. Nathan also knew that God had forgiven David (2 Samuel 12) but that there would be consequences for his behavior.

Christians may never realize how many times God has given them information that no one on earth could know and has given them insight that they never would have thought of naturally. God is omniscient and can reveal His knowledge to his servants in the church when they ask for it.

Peter knew that Ananias and Sapphira were lying to the Holy Spirit concerning a cash gift they wanted to give to the church (Acts 5:1–10). The gift appeared legitimate, and they were doing what several others had already done. However, when Ananias presented his money to Peter, Peter said, "Ananias, how is it that Satan has so filled your heart that you have lied to the Holy Spirit and have kept for yourself some of the money you received for the land?" (Acts 5:3). Peter had a knowledge that did not come from a person, a book, or a document; no one had given him this information. The Holy Spirit had revealed it to him.

You might be a supervisor or employee who has to "know" something in order to be more effective on your job. God can supernaturally reveal His eternal truths about your situation in order for you to be creative and do your job with greater expertise. God desires to give you knowledge about your spiritual ministry and in the practical areas of your everyday life as well. Just ask Him for wisdom. (See James 1:5.)

FAITH

The faith that Paul is speaking of here is different from the faith that everyone needs for salvation. All people can have enough "salvation faith," which is also a gift of God, to believe in Christ, His physical resurrection, and His atonement for their sins. The Bible tells us that "without faith it is impossible to please God" (Heb. 11:6), and that "the righteous will live by faith" (Rom. 1:17).

This manifestation of faith that Paul lists is unique to certain individuals in the body of Christ. It can be called a "special faith." On the day that Elijah challenged the prophets of Baal to cry out to their gods for a miracle, he demonstrated a unique faith. He mocked these false leaders saying, "Let's see which of our gods answers prayer" (1 Kings 18:24). After watching them publicly humiliate themselves for hours, Elijah cried out to God for fire to fall from heaven and consume the sacrifice he had prepared. Immediately the sacrifice was consumed, thus proving that Elijah's God was the real God. (See 1 Kings 18:36–39.)

Peter demonstrated unusual faith when he knew that a crippled beggar would be healed. (Acts 3:1–7). When the ship that Paul was on was about to sink in a terrible storm, Paul had a unique faith that everyone would survive. Perhaps you have known someone who has a faith that rises above normal. It is usually accompanied with great boldness, tenacity, and courage in spite of the odds.

GIFTS OF HEALING

This gift has been greatly misunderstood by many. Some have thought that if a person has this gift, everyone for whom the person prays should be healed. Tragically, some ministries have tried to manipulate people into thinking that people were healed when they were not. This particular gift can bring a great deal of attention to the person who has it—or to the one who pretends to have it. We need to remember that since this is a gift of God, He does the healing and He should receive all the glory for it. When a doctor is involved, we should be grateful for the doctor's assistance but give God the glory for the doctor's expertise and the healing that results.

We should also understand that not all are healed when they are prayed for (for reasons God only knows), and we can trust our merciful God with the reasons and the results. It is the will of God to heal unless there is a higher purpose to be achieved from the ailment. We can trust Him to do what is eternally best in our lives and in the lives of those for whom we pray. Timothy apparently had difficulty with his stomach. (See 1 Timothy 5:23.) Paul left a traveling companion named Trophimus at Miletus because he was sick (2 Tim. 4:20). Paul himself had a "thorn in the flesh" that many believe was a physical battle with which he struggled. In Paul's case, he understood that God chose not to heal him of this particular problem. He explained the situation this way, "Three times I pleaded with the Lord to take it away from me. But he said to me, 'My grace is sufficient for you, for my power is made perfect in weakness'" (2 Cor. 12:8–9). Paul had seen astonishing miracles in his life; however, on this particular occasion it was God's will that the "thorn" remain. Paul said that God wanted "to keep me from becoming conceited because of these surpassingly great revelations" (2 Cor. 12:7).

Healing is to be part of the life of the church. Not only are there those who have a special gift in this area, but James also tells us, "Is any one of you sick? He should call the elders of the church to pray over him and anoint him with oil in the name of the Lord. And the prayer offered in faith will make the sick person well" (James 5:14–15). On many occasions I have seen people healed because the church has obeyed this Scripture.

If a healing has truly taken place, it should be verifiable by professionals and by friends who have known the healed individual.

MIRACULOUS POWERS

I have often thought about the time when the disciples heard Jesus say to them, "I tell you the truth, anyone who has faith in me will do what I have been doing. He will do even greater things than these" (John 14:12). The disciples had watched Jesus feed several thousand people with a little boy's lunch. They had seen Him heal people of illnesses, cast out demons, and even raise the dead. They had watched Him walk on water. At the time when Jesus told them they would "do even greater things than these," they must have wondered, "What in the world could He be talking about? He is the Son of God, and we are only people."

After the Day of Pentecost, the issue was cleared up. These disciples saw the promise fulfilled. Peter raised a lady named Tabitha to life (Acts 9:40). A boy who had died from falling three stories out of a building was healed when Paul "threw himself on the young man and put his arms around him" (Acts 20:10). The Bible tells us that "God did extraordinary miracles through Paul, so that even handkerchiefs and aprons that had touched him were taken to the sick, and their illnesses were cured and the evil spirits left them" (Acts 19:11–12). At one time people laid the sick in the streets so that Peter's shadow would pass over them. (See Acts 5:15.) Scripture says that "the apostles performed many miraculous signs and wonders among the people" (Acts 9:12).

In describing miracles, Donald Gee explains, "The literal Greek of the passage is dunamis, 'operation of works of power.' The great thought is of power; the power of God operating by the Spirit of God in and through the church of God."[21] A miracle to us is not an impossible task to God. It is natural for God to perform a miracle. After all, he spoke this world and everything we see, smell, hear, touch, and taste into existence. God can interrupt the natural order of things and perform a miracle if He chooses.

When God uses someone with this gift, a surge of faith rises up from within that person because a seemingly impossible situation changes, a closed door opens, an angelic visitation occurs, or even nature, as we understand it changes. Thus, all miracles should bring glory to God.

PROPHECY

Prophecy is a divinely inspired utterance in the speaker's and hearer's language. It could be, but is not necessarily, part of a pastor's sermon. Often the gift of prophecy is part of a person's life (it is what he or she is known for) within the church body. The Scripture tells us that "Philip the evangelist...had four unmarried daughters who prophesied" (Acts 21:8–9). Also, there was "a prophet named Agabus" (v. 10) who warned Paul of his future imprisonment in Jerusalem. This unique gift of the Spirit illuminates a kingdom principle. It can be predictive or can even specifically reveal the spiritual condition of a person's heart. Theologian Stanley Horton has said, "As speaking with tongues is a supernatural utterance in an unknown tongue, so prophesy is a supernatural utterance in a known tongue. It is a manifestation of the Spirit of God, and not of the human mind."[22]

Because there is always the possibility of a person telling someone or a church group something they want them to hear (not necessarily what God wants them to hear), or telling something with a wrong attitude, we are instructed in the Scripture to "weigh carefully what is said" (1 Cor. 14:29). This is done by asking ourselves questions like, is what the person said biblical? Was it encouraging, strengthening, and comforting to the church? (See 1 Corinthians 14:3.) It is ideal when the individual or the church body knows the person because he or she is a part of the church. The gift of discernment is helpful as well when judging a prophecy.

DISTINGUISHING BETWEEN SPIRITS

In a world where evil spirits are deceiving people and distracting them from the truth, we desperately need the gift of discernment. Satan uses his demons to distort God's truth, confuse God's people, and blind those without Christ. It is absolutely necessary to understand who Satan is and how he operates as the enemy of our souls.[23] Distinguishing between spirits will enable us to understand Satan's strategy and detect his messengers who are trying to ruin the church.

L. Thomas Holdcroft said, "By means of this gift, human natural senses are supplemented by appropriate divine powers, so that humans are able to relate in understanding in the spirit world. The gift of discerning of spirits does not enable one to discern people; it is not 'discernment' in the abstract, but simply what it purports to be: the discerning of analytic classification and judgment of spirits."[24]

The gift of discernment was used when Paul was followed by a girl who shouted, "These men are servants of the Most High God, who are telling you the way to be saved" (Acts 16:17). Even though she was saying words that were correct, Paul sensed that she had a demon spirit that enabled her to predict the future (remember, Satan is a counterfeiter of true gifts). He let this girl "do her thing" for several days, then "finally Paul became so troubled that he turned around and said to the spirit, 'In the name of Jesus Christ I command you to come out of her!' At that moment the spirit left her" (Acts 16:18).

Peter used discernment to protect the church from deceit and manipulation when he recognized the lie Ananias and Sapphira tired to tell the church (Acts 5). Peter also stopped a man with a wicked heart from deluding the church by trying to buy the gift of the baptism in the Holy Spirit. (See Acts 8:14–23.)

We have often prayed for this gift because we understand that our world can be very complicated and confusing because of Satan's involvement. It is critical that we interpret with God's understanding both the clear truth in life and the people who have influence on our lives.

SPEAKING IN DIFFERENT KINDS OF TONGUES

The gift of speaking in an unknown tongue is generally used for private worship or for praying with our spirit. (See 1 Corinthians 14:2–4.) It is the gift of speaking supernaturally in a language not known to the individual.[25] The Bible tells us that this practice will edify us. When we pray in tongues, our spirit prays a vertical prayer or offers worship up to God.

When someone gives a message in tongues at a church gathering, God inspires a person's spirit to speak of the "wonders of God" (Acts 2:11), to edify and encourage the church, or to specifically reveal the secrets of someone's heart. (See 1 Corinthians 14:25.) This gift will then be used in a horizontal way.

God is interested in bringing edification to the whole church. With that concern, he has given some the ability to give a message in tongues with the expectation that either they or someone else will interpret the utterance. In his article in *The Full Life Study Bible,* Donald Stamps writes:

This gift has two main purposes:

1. Speaking in tongues accompanied by interpretation is used in public worship services to communicate the Spirit-directed worship, praise, or prophecy (1 Cor. 14:5–6, 13–17);

2. Speaking in tongues is used by the believer to speak to God in his or her personal devotions and thus to build up one's spiritual life (1 Cor. 14:4).[26]

Paul tells us that speaking in tongues is a sign for unbelievers when it is accompanied by an interpretation. (See 1 Corinthians 14:22–33.) He also says that when God inspires a person or persons to give a message in tongues (or prophecy), only two or "at the most three" (vv. 27, 29) messages should be given. This gift has its proper place in the worship service; however, it seems that the Corinthians had occasions where their services had more than three messages. The leadership of the church needs to discern what is of God and what is of human flesh. While we don't want to prevent the Spirit of God from doing His will in a worship service, we also need to be sensitive to the timing of a message in tongues, the person giving the message, and the number of messages given in one service. Paul said, "God is not a God of disorder but of peace" (v. 33).

INTERPRETATION OF TONGUES

Persons who have the gift of interpretation of tongues have the ability to interpret what another person or they have said in an unknown tongue. David Lim comments:

Why do we need two gifts that must accompany one another? The answer lies in the nature of tongues. The Holy Spirit touches our spirit. We desire to praise God. We find liberation to exalt God's goodness in our lives. One may be exalting God over a great theological truth about his character, his redemptive work, or his special care of us... The challenge from the speaker to the Body in his utterance in tongues is, "Let God touch your spirit the way He has touched my spirit!" Hocken says, "If the gift of tongues is fuller praise of God, the reception of this gift necessarily means a deeper knowledge of God."

When the interpretation allows the congregation to understand what is being said, they are encouraged to worship. So even though tongues has this horizontal dimension, its purpose is to lead the Body to (vertical) worship.[27]

HOW ARE YOU GIFTED?

The gifts of the Spirit are not just for church leaders; they are for everyone in the body of Christ, and the need for these nine gifts is more immediate today than perhaps at any other time in the history of the church. You have an integral part in the body, and God wants to use you. The work of the Holy Spirit is in the manifestation of the supernatural, in miracles, and in signs and wonders. As we become more aware of the Holy Spirit's work and our hearts become more open to it, we will experience a greater dimension of the supernatural with its gifts and manifestations.

Shortly after the wall fell between Eastern and Western Europe, I was invited to speak in one of Europe's largest evangelical churches, which is located in Timisoara, Romania. This Pentecostal church of several thousand had gone through many trials and much persecution, but the pressure only made it stronger. The pastor of the church is Teodor Codreanu, a humble yet powerful Christian leader in that country.

I remember that day well. On the Sunday that I was to minister, I was somewhat nervous because of being in a strange country, and I hoped to be able to communicate my message effectively through the translator. I sincerely wanted to encourage this wonderful congregation and can remember the feeling I had while preaching. I felt God's presence and His power working through me in an unusual way. The sermon went smoothly, and the translator seemed to be right with me. I felt that the people were understanding me and that the Lord was speaking His truth through His Word. Actually, I felt as comfortable there as I had in the church near Seattle where I pastored at the time. When I finished, numerous people gave their lives to Christ. I was grateful for God's help.

After the service something happened that I did not expect. Pastor Codreanu came to me and said that someone in his congregation had a message from God for me. Frankly, I am a little suspicious when someone says this, but I had such respect and trust for this pastor that I said, "Good, I would like to hear it."

Pastor Codreanu took me to the side of the platform, and there stood a girl who was perhaps twelve to fifteen years old. The pastor said to me, "This is the person. She has a message from God for you."

I was somewhat surprised as I thought it would be an older person, perhaps a deacon or another pastor.

The young girl shyly looked at me and quietly began speaking through the translator. She said that while I was speaking, she had seen a vision. I gently said, "Please tell me what you saw."

The little girl told me, "While you were speaking, there appeared two hands above your head. The hands pointed down toward your head and oil dripped from them on you." She continued, "I'm not sure about the meaning of the vision, but I know that God wanted me to tell you what I saw."

What this little girl saw was exactly what I needed to hear. I desperately craved God's anointing to be on me that day. This vision confirmed to me that He had heard my heart's desire and answered my prayer. God had used a little girl in the body of Christ to bless me. The gift of the Holy Spirit had brought great encouragement to me.

Your God-given gifts are needed as well. They are to be used to serve the body of Christ and to enable you to be effective in the ministry God has given you.

Chapter 7

THE EXPERIENCE:
WHAT MUST I DO?

A s THE WORSHIP portion of the morning service pro-
gressed, I observed that most of the people sensed a
tremendous presence of God in the sanctuary. Some
had their hands lifted into the air signifying submission of
their lives to the Lord, and others lifted their hands in praise as
though He were standing in front of them. Tears flowed down
the cheeks of many as the gentle breeze of the Holy Spirit
moved throughout the congregation. Like a skilled surgeon,
the worship leader was carefully leading the congregation in
choruses they knew by heart mixed with songs from the hym-
nbook. He sincerely desired that the people offer pure praise
and adoration to God and so avoided any hint of crowd or
psychological manipulation.

In a few moments I would be speaking to this hungry
group of people. As I was worshiping God and at the same
time observing the people, I sensed a very distinct impression: "During the altar service, God is going to do wonderful
things."

I doubted the thought, rationalizing that it was only my
imagination, but it was so clear that I instinctively knew that
it could be the voice of the Holy Spirit. In fact, a tremendous
faith, along with curiosity of what God would do, grew in my
heart as I gave the message to the people.

When I was done speaking, I asked those who desired to

accept Christ as their Savior to come to the front of the sanctuary. Many people responded from all over the building. I then asked those who had desperate situations in their lives and wanted special prayer to come to the front of the church so the deacons and elders could pray for them. The altar portion of the packed, thousand-seat sanctuary became filled with people, so much so that the aisles of the church became full as well. The same sweet presence of the Lord had remained in the building from the beginning of the worship. My mind went back to what I felt the Holy Spirit had communicated to me earlier in the service, "I am going to do wonderful things."

In spite of there being hundreds of people down front, a young teenage girl and her mother caught my attention. They carefully worked their way through the crowd, the mother tenderly leading her young daughter toward me. As they got closer, I noticed that the girl had Down's syndrome. As I prayed for several other people, it became apparent that this pair wanted to speak to me.

The mother introduced herself and her daughter to me and quickly added that the young girl had accepted Christ just a few weeks before. She then added, "My daughter would like you to pray for her that she would receive the baptism in the Holy Spirit." I briefly spoke to the girl, noticing that her physical difficulty prevented her from speaking clearly. However, she could speak in short sentences with limited vocabulary.

"Honey, do you love Jesus with all of your heart?" I asked her.

She immediately replied, "Yes, I do!"

I asked her, "Are you going to serve Him for all of your life?"

"Yes, for all of my life," she responded.

"Do you want Jesus to baptize you in the Holy Spirit?" I asked.

With a hungry look in her eyes and determination in her voice, she said, "Yes."

I gently put my hands on her little shoulders and prayed that God would baptize her in the Holy Spirit. I instructed her

128

to pray after me, "Jesus, I love You and want You to baptize me in the Holy Spirit."

She said, "Jesus, I love You. Please baptize me in the Holy Spirit."

I then instructed her to worship God with her voice and the words God would give her.[1]

I have seen this happen hundreds of times before, but this experience in particular touched me. She immediately began worshiping God in a language she had never learned. Her hands were lifted into the air, her eyes were closed, and she was speaking in this new language with a clarity that she did not have in her English language. She was overjoyed with what God was doing for her.

As I turned and walked toward another person who desired prayer, I thought, God does not show favoritism. His salvation by grace and His powerful baptism are for "whomsoever." It does not matter whether a person is intelligent, handicapped, old, or young. God wants all people in his church to receive all that he has for them.[2]

As a born-again Christian you are special to God. You are His child. You are part of God's kingdom and no longer in the dominion of darkness. (See Colossians 1:13.) After your decision to make Christ your Savior, the choice to receive the baptism in the Holy Spirit can be your next decision. As we said earlier, this experience does not make you more special, nor will it cause God to love you more. God has no favorite people in His kingdom, only some who have unique roles. The baptism in the Holy Spirit will give you all the power you need to do all that God has asked of you. God has offered this baptism to you because He wants to give you the same power He gave the early church. Evangelist Reinhard Bonnke says, "If we receive the same baptism, it must have the same effect. Jesus the Baptizer has not changed, nor have His methods. In God's kingdom we are not copies of copies, but originals from The Original, Jesus Christ. When we experience the baptism in the Holy Sprit, we do not receive leftovers, but the original experience."[3]

Every Christian is to be a witness. We are not all evangelists, but we have a responsibility to evangelize. We are to live the Christian life in front of people and tell them about the gospel of Jesus Christ. The baptism in the Holy Spirit will enable you to do this. "The baptism in the Spirit means that people, saved by grace, and born again can have new experiences and become Spirit-energized witnesses for Christ."[4]

After Jesus Christ was resurrected He told His disciples to "wait for the gift my Father promised" (Acts 1:4). This gift is for every believer in the world today. You may disagree with us on some points of terminology and perhaps some theology, but we hope that we all hold this one thing in common— namely, that we want a deeper, richer, more powerful experience of God's Spirit. You might call it "baptism," "fullness," or the "infilling of the Holy Spirit." Whatever your terminology, we pray that you experience it.[5]

I did not become a Christian until I was twenty-one years old. A missionary told me about Christ while I was serving in the military on Guam. Before my born-again experience, I was involved in many destructive behaviors. I had a dynamic conversion in which God also delivered me from alcohol, smoking, cursing, and confusion about the meaning of life. I was astounded with what God had done for me. Shortly after I became a Christian, the missionary told me that there was another experience I could enjoy—the promised baptism in the Holy Spirit. I could not imagine how there could be more, since I was already so grateful for all that God had done for me. But I hungered for all that God had to offer and asked God to give me this experience.

A few days later I was on duty in a highly secure military facility handling secret and top secret messages. As I sensed the presence of God come over me, I wondered what was going on. I felt a closeness to God, similar to what I felt when praying in church, only more intense. I knew that God was doing something very special even in the highly secular environment.

As soon as I finished my duty shift, I went to another Christian's home. When I explained that I had sensed God's presence in a unique way, we began to pray together and worship God. Almost immediately I began to speak in a language I had never learned. That night God baptized me with the Holy Spirit.

Every person who has received this experience can tell you his or her unique story about how it happened. Some, like the house of Cornelius (see Acts 10), received the experience within seconds after their conversion. Others may have been Christians for decades without ever having heard that there was such an experience. The point is not so much *when* you hear of this tremendous promise or *how* you receive it; it is that you take advantage of all that God has for you.

Some people have tried to say that the baptism in the Spirit with signs following was only for the early disciples who needed the extra "charge" or unique gifting to get Christianity started. Well, we need it too! It is critical that we utilize every available bit of energy and supernatural strength to do God's work in an evil world.

God's power is for you and me today. His wonderful gift is available to us just as it was to the early church. You can receive the same power with signs following that the early church received. There simply is no biblical support for the opinions of some who say this experience is not for us. It is for today, and it can be a part of your life. D. L. Moody said, "God commands us to be filled with the Spirit; and if we aren't filled, it's because we're living beneath our privileges."[6] Peter said to the thousands of onlookers, "The promise is for you and your children and for all who are far off—for all whom the Lord our God will call" (Acts 2:39).

Let us examine Peter's words. First, he said the promise is "for you." The people whom Peter was talking to were the same ones he had accused of putting Jesus to death by "nailing him to the cross" (Acts 2:23). The very people responsible for killing Jesus were being offered the gift of the baptism in the Holy Spirit. God wanted them to know that he would forgive them if they repented, and he would give the same experience that the 120 had received in the Upper Room. (See Acts 1:13; 2:1.)

Second, Peter said the promise is for "your children." It is to be passed on from generation to generation. Christianity is not a one-generation religion. God has no grandchildren, only children. Also, God does not want us to think that this experience was only for people many generations ago. Peter was telling his listeners that this promise was for their children, grandchildren, great-grandchildren, and so on. Paul prayed for a group of Ephesian disciples to receive the baptism in the Holy Spirit approximately twenty years after the original disciples had had the experience. (See Acts 19:1–7.) The word "children" not only means our immediate families, but also our descendants. We are descendants of the early church. Their experience can be ours.

Third, Peter said the promise is for "all who are far off" (Acts 2:39). Perhaps he was prophetically speaking about the Christians who would be alive when the rapture of the church occurred. Looking down through the ages, Peter's spiritual eyes may have had a glimpse of today's church. We are "far off" in time and space.

Fourth, Peter said the promise is "for all whom the Lord our God will call" (Acts 2:39). God's call to salvation is for everyone. He "wants all men to be saved and come to a knowledge of the truth" (1 Tim. 2:4). Jesus said, "No one can come to me unless the Father who sent me draws him" (John 6:44). He later added, "No one can come to me unless the Father had enabled him" (v. 65). The Father draws us to Jesus, and the Father has given the guarantee that not only would those who come to Christ receive salvation, but "the promise" would be available to them too. We who have salvation are the ones the "Lord our

God will call" (Acts 2:39). You can have your own personal experience. In fact, God does not want you to just watch those who have had powerful experiences in the Lord. He wants this baptism for you just as much as he does for anyone else.

HOW TO RECEIVE THE FULLNESS OF THE HOLY SPIRIT

1. Remember that the Holy Spirit is "holy."

He will not enter a vessel that is unclean. Only Christians, those who have been forgiven, receive this experience. It belongs to no other religion and cannot occur unless the person's heart has been purified by accepting Jesus as his or her personal Lord and Savior. You might think that you will never be clean enough. Yes, you will; you only need to give your life to Jesus, ask Him to forgive you of your sins, and repent of (stop) your wrong behavior. Peter said, "Repent, then, and turn to God, so that your sins may be wiped out, that times of refreshing may come from the Lord" (Acts 3:19). He also said, "Repent...for the forgiveness of your sins. And you will receive the gift of the Holy Spirit" (Acts 2:38).

John reminds us "the blood of Jesus, his [God's] Son, purifies us from all sin" (1 John 1:7). But you must be sure you are wholly committed to him. As D. L. Moody said, "If we are full of pride and conceit and ambition and self-seeking and pleasure and the world, there is no room for the Spirit of God, and I believe many a man is praying to God to fill him when he is full already with something else."[7] And Charles Spurgeon said:

> The Holy Spirit makes no promise to bless compromises. If we make a treaty with error or sin, we do it at our own risk. If we do anything that we are not clear about, if we tamper with truth or holiness, if we are friends of the world, if we make provision for the flesh, if we preach half-heartedly and are in league with terrorists, we have no promise that the Holy Spirit will go with us. If you

want to know what great things the Lord can do, as the Lord God Almighty, be separate from the world, and from those who apostatize from the truth. The man of God will have nothing to do with Sodom, or with false doctrine. If you see anything that is evil, give it the cut direct. Have done with those who have done with the truth.[8]

2. Understand that this gift is for you.

You have nothing to fear from the gifts and blessings that God has offered you. Just as He gave the baptism in the Holy Spirit to the early disciples, He desires for you to have it. It will help you, not hurt you, because the One who has created you knows what you need.

Some are afraid of the experience because they grew up in a denomination that has been critical of the baptism in the Holy Spirit. He or she may have seen excesses or other unwise behavior by some and thought they were unbalanced people. You may even have tried to pray for this experience yourself and felt that it did not work.

Know that God is not a God of confusion, and He truly understands your many concerns. You have nothing to fear from any of the gifts He has for you. As we mentioned earlier, Jesus said, "Which of you fathers, if your son asks for a fish, will give him a snake instead? Or if he asks for an egg, will give him a scorpion? If you then, though you are evil, know how to give good gifts to your children, how much more will your Father in heaven give the Holy Spirit to those who ask him!" (Luke 11:11–13). This passage is not referring to the impartation of the Spirit into the life of the new believer at the moment he or she is born again (John 3:3); it is speaking about the blessing of the baptism in the Holy Spirit that Jesus promised to His disciples.

John the Baptist prophesied that Jesus would baptize His followers in the Holy Spirit. (See Matthew 3:11; Mark 1:8; Luke 3:16; John 1:33.) Jesus also spoke prophetically when he said, "In a few days you will be baptized with the Holy Spirit" (Acts

1:5; 11:16). In the Acts passages above, Jesus promised to give the Holy Spirit to everyone who asked. His promise was first fulfilled at Pentecost and is available for you and me today.

3. Hunger for all that God has for you.

A. W. Tozer said, "Before we can be filled with the Spirit, the desire to be filled must be all-consuming. It must be for the time the biggest thing in life, so acute, so intrusive to crowd out everything else. The degree of fullness in any life accords perfectly with the intensity of true desire. We have as much of God as we acutely desire"[9]

There must be a holy ambition, a desire for more of Jesus, and a pure devotion in our hearts when we seek anything from God. There can be no impure motivations or any desire to have this gift so that we can use it for our own benefit. It is for God's benefit, and we must hunger to glorify Him in all that we do. Jesus said "Blessed are those who hunger and thirst for righteousness, for they will be filled" (Matt. 5:6).

4. Ask God to baptize you with the Holy Spirit.

I have known some who have received the baptism in the Holy Spirit at the time of their salvation. I believe that God saw their hungry hearts crying out for everything He had to offer. Others have come to this experience decades after their born-again experience. For whatever reason, they did not ask for it. Perhaps they doubted the reality of it or the need for it. Only God knows the reasons.

If you want to receive the baptism in the Holy Spirit, we encourage you to schedule a time to be alone with God or to attend a Bible study group or church where this experience is common, and ask Jesus to baptize you in the Holy Spirit.

5. Believe that God will give you the promise by faith.

The Bible tells us "without faith it is impossible to please God, because anyone who comes to him must believe that he exists and that he rewards those who earnestly seek him" (Heb. 11:6). Our salvation comes to us because we have faith in the resurrected Jesus Christ. Likewise, we receive the baptism in the Holy Spirit by believing that God will give us the promise. Jesus said, "'If anyone is thirsty, let him come to me and drink. Whoever believes in me, as the Scripture has said, streams of living water will flow from within him.' By this he meant the Spirit, whom those who believed in him were later to receive" (John 7:37–39). Faith means accepting what God has offered to you. You do not need to add anything to your salvation experience or try to persuade Jesus that you are good enough to receive this gift. Because you are a child of God, you can approach Him with courage and boldness.

When my wife and I give birthday gifts to our grandchildren, we simply present the gifts to them, and they in turn reach out their hands and take the gifts. We are eager to give, and they are happy to receive. They do not need to beg, recite something, or wait for another day. And so it is with God's gift of the promised baptism in the Holy Spirit. It brings great pleasure to God to give you this blessing, and you can just take it by faith.

6. By faith, worship God in the language He gives you.

You can have the ability to speak in tongues just as the early disciples spoke in a language they had never learned when they received "the blessing." Paul tells us that when we speak in tongues we do not speak to people but to God, and that our spirit is praying. (See 1 Corinthians 14:2.) If you are hesitant, pray in your native tongue, worshiping God for a time; then ask God to help you speak in the language He has given you. It may be only one word or it may be a sentence, but by faith you begin speaking in a language you have never learned.

When you begin praying in the unknown tongue (language) that God gives you, remember that your spirit is praying. The devil has no idea what you are saying, but God understands the language of your spirit. Reinhard Bonnke says, "Tongues is the only language the devil cannot understand. The archconfuser is totally confused himself, because he does not even know the alphabet of the Holy Spirit. Satan cannot crack the Holy Spirit's secret code which puts us in touch with the throne of heaven."[10]

You might not know what you are saying to God, but you can sense that you are communicating to him from your heart. Most of us have had times when we simply did not know how to verbalize what we wanted to pray about but felt the concern, or burden, to pray. God helps us during these times by enabling us to speak in the language given to us by the Holy Spirit or perhaps just by groaning from our hearts. The Lord hears these languages of the heart. Paul said, "The Spirit helps us in our weakness. We do not know what we ought to pray for, but the Spirit himself intercedes for us with groans that words cannot express" (Rom. 8:26).

John Harper made a true analogy when he said, "Tongues is a heart language. As a baby lies in his mother's arms and babbles to his mother—they both understand what he means. So we lie in God's arms and babble to him. And we both understand."[11] The only exception that I take with this statement is that speaking in tongues is not babble. It is a language that God miraculously gives. Our bodies are "temples[s] of the Holy Spirit" (1 Cor. 6:19), and our "temples" are to be houses of prayer. When we pray in the language that the Holy Spirit gives us, we communicate pure, powerful prayers to the very throne of God. The Spirit who dwells in us loves to pray, and when we are full of the Holy Spirit, we have a great desire to pray.

7. Live by the Spirit.

To live by the Spirit is to live as Jesus lived. Every day you can choose to live a holy life, to be sensitive to God's will, and to serve God with all your heart. Those who have been baptized in the Holy Spirit will desire to please Jesus in all they do.

After years of researching people who had received the baptism in the Holy Spirit, John Sherrill noted:

Of all the variety of experiences with the Holy Spirit, one thing held true in every case. Whether the baptism came quietly or with a bang, unexpectedly or after long seeking, the ultimate result was to draw the individual closer to Christ. Jesus was no longer a figure on the pages of a history book. Nor, even, a memory from some personal mountaintop experience. His Spirit was with the Baptized believer in a present-time, minute-by-minute way, showing him at every turn the nature and personality of Christ.[12]

Oswald Chambers rightfully said, "There is one thing we cannot imitate: we cannot imitate being full of the Holy Ghost."[13] It is a great concern to me when I see or hear of people who claim to be full of God's precious Holy Spirit but live a life that is displeasing to God. It does not matter what kind of miraculous experiences a person seems to demonstrate, how much they speak in tongues, or what kind of power they seem to demonstrate—if they do not glorify Jesus in the way they live and the things they say, they are not full of the Holy Spirit. They are either deceived or are trying to manipulate people. Such behavior is a mockery to our holy God. We will speak about this more in the next chapter. Here, however, we must remind ourselves that we are not to "believe every spirit, but test the spirits to see whether they are from God, because many false prophets have gone out into the world" (1 John 4:1). One of the ways we know someone is not of God is that he or she does not act like Jesus or live a life that demonstrates that the Holy Spirit lives in him or her. When people live by the Spirit, they have a tender heart toward the things of God and are sensitive to the needs of others. Their lifestyle will include repentance, forgiveness, holiness, sensitivity to the things of God, boldness, courage, and power.

A life of repentance
Paul tells us that our sinful nature will battle against the

Spirit who lives in us. (See Galatians 5:16–26.) With this battle going on, we frequently need to repent of our attitude, conversation, or actions. We can live a life that pleases the Holy Spirit; however, if we sin, we need to repent. John said, "My dear children, I write this to you so that you will not sin. But if anybody does sin, we have one who speaks to the Father in our defense—Jesus Christ, the Righteous One" (1 John 2:1). D. L. Moody said, "Man is born with his back toward God. When he truly repents, he turns right around and faces God. Repentance is a change of mind. . . . Repentance is the tear in the eye of faith."[14]

A life of forgiveness

When we walk in the Spirit, we are both asking people to forgive us for something we have said or done and we are forgiving people for what they have done against us. The Spirit-filled life is a life in which we seek forgiveness from God (and He forgives), we seek forgiveness from others, and we forgive others. Someone has said that every great marriage is made up of two great forgivers. A great church is made up of a lot of great forgivers.

When Andrew Jackson was being interviewed for church membership, the pastor said, "General, there is one more question which I must ask you. Can you forgive all your enemies?"

General Jackson was silent as he recalled his stormy life of bitter fighting. Then he responded, "My political enemies I can freely forgive; but as for those who attacked me for serving my country and those who slandered my wife—Doctor, I cannot forgive them!"

The pastor made it clear to Jackson that before he could become a member of that church and partake of the broken bread and the cup, his hatred and bitterness must be confessed and dealt with before God.

Again there was an awkward silence. Then Jackson affirmed that if God would help him, he would forgive his enemies.[15]

Forgivers and those who ask for forgiveness are "big people" who serve a God who is a big forgiver.

A life of holiness

When we walk in the Spirit, we live a life that is different from the world we live in. We do not get caught up in the fads of this world but keep our lives pure. We are in the kingdom of God, not the dominion of darkness. The Holy Spirit will make us feel sensitive to what we say and do. He will guide our consciences and help us to know what is displeasing to God. With every relationship, decision, and thought, He will help us to know what is Christ honoring.

A life of sensitivity to the things of God

Paul tells us, "The Spirit searches all things, even the deep things of God. For who among men knows the thoughts of a man except the man's spirit within him? In the same way no one knows the thoughts of God except the Spirit of God. We have not received the spirit of the world but the Spirit who is from God, that we may understand what God has freely given us" (1 Cor. 2:10–12). In this portion of Scripture, Paul explains that the Spirit of God will reveal to believers God's deep promises. Every day He will make us aware of God's will and His plan for our lives.

A life of boldness, courage, and power

I have seen shy people become extroverted and bold in their faith when they are walking in the Spirit. I have watched people who struggled with fear become courageous in their lives and in their faith. I have watched little children witness to mature adults with great confidence. The Spirit-led life is one of boldness and courage. Samuel Chadwick said, "To the church, Pentecost brought light, power, joy. There came to each illumination of mind, assurance of heart, intensity of love, fullness of power, exuberance of joy. No one needed to ask if they had received the Holy Ghost. Fire is self-evident. So is power!"[16]

When Peter and John were warned not to speak or teach in

the name of Jesus, they responded by going to the Christian community and telling them about the threats. Undoubtedly they were concerned about what might happen to them, but their response to the warnings did not paralyze them with fear or slow them down in the least. Instead of stopping, they prayed for more boldness to continue preaching and teaching about Jesus. They prayed:

> Now, Lord, consider their threats and enable your servants to speak your word with great boldness. Stretch out your hand to heal and perform miraculous sings and wonders through the name of your holy servant Jesus.
>
> After they prayed, the place where they were meeting was shaken. And they were all filled with the Holy Spirit and spoke the word of God boldly.
>
> —ACTS 4:29–31

God will enable you to live a life full of courage and power. On many occasions I have felt fearful or nervous about a situation I was facing. On these occasions I have turned to God in prayer and asked Him for boldness and strength to face the time. He has never let me down. Paul instructed Timothy, his son in the faith, that "God did not give us a spirit of timidity, but a spirit of power, of love and of self-discipline" (2 Tim. 1:7). Through the Holy Spirit, you can have spiritual power that is greater than human strength.

THE STORY OF DR. WILLIS C. HOOVER

At the turn of the nineteenth century, Willis C. Hoover, a medical doctor in Chicago, and his wife decided to apply for a missionary appointment with the Methodist Episcopal Church and move to Chile. At that time they did not realize that God would use them to build a growing congregation of eight hundred and then send a revival that would affect millions in Chile during the twentieth century.

Dr. Hoover had heard of the 1906 Azusa Street outpouring in Los Angeles. Hoover's grandson recalls, "The revival fired his interest and he began studying the Bible in earnest.... He called his family together for special times of prayer for revival."

One night during a prayer meeting while Hoover knelt on the platform, he was startled to hear people praying in a united prayer, unlike the Methodist custom. Then when the Holy Spirit descended in a special manner, the congregation spoke in tongues. A desire to evangelize came to the congregation, and they began to go throughout the community telling people about the gospel of Jesus Christ.

The news of what was happening got to Hoover's superiors, and he was ordered to cease Pentecostal activities and the teaching of the Pentecostal doctrines or he would be dismissed from the church. Hoover's mind went back to the sixteenth century, to Martin Luther, who took a stand he believed was right. Hoover said, "Here I stand," echoing Luther; "God help me. I cannot do otherwise." Approximately four hundred members of the church left with him and formed the Methodist Pentecostal Church.

Hoover lost his American financial support, walked away from the denomination he loved, and held on to the belief that God gave him and his congregation a precious promise. His grandson said, "He never wavered in his belief that the 1909 revival had come from heaven."

When Willis Hoover lay dying in 1936, he prayed for another great revival. Today millions upon millions of people have received "the blessing" throughout Chile and the rest of Latin America.[17] It can be your experience too.

Chapter 8

THE DANGERS: EXCESSES AND EXTREMES

ELIGIOUS CHARLATANS AND their hoaxes have fascinated Americans almost as much as genuine miracles."[1] People want so badly to see something supernatural that they will believe almost anything.

A few years ago a notorious so-called faith healer and evangelist was caught in the act of tricking people into thinking that he was healing members of his audience. A reporter for *U.S. News and World Report* wrote:

> Probably the most renowned exposure of a hoax in recent years was in 1986, when an investigative team led by magician James Randi challenged the "divine gifts" claimed by well-known faith healer Peter Popoff. At his peak in the mid 80s, Popoff appeared on more than fifty TV stations and collected about $550,000 a month from followers who were amazed at his "powers." During his services, Popoff approached total strangers, calling out their names and addresses and then diagnosing their illnesses. He attributed his abilities to the Holy Spirit, but Randi discovered that, like the movie character Reverend Nightengale, Popoff had some help from a tiny radio receiver concealed in his ear. Popoff's wife, Elizabeth, and other aides gathered personal details from audience members before the service began, then relayed them to the evangelist via his earphone. After Randi played tapes

of the scam on "The Tonight Show," Popoff's contributions dried up and he filed for bankruptcy.[2]

Religious fakes are of great concern to me. Not only are they mocking real supernatural healings and miracles but also they are taking advantage of people's pain and suffering. Many attend their meetings fully expecting that they will receive an answer for the crisis in their lives. Some come with physical, even terminal, illnesses, and some are in great need of financial miracles. Many come because they are in agony from a devastating relationship or are desperately hungry to relate to a supernatural God. For whatever reason, they come—sometimes by the thousands—the curious, the hungry, and the needy. Sadly, some very evil people take advantage of human suffering, even in religious services. Peter tells us that people like this "will be paid back with harm for the harm they have done" (2 Peter 2:13).

In the same article, *U.S. News and World Report* stated:

> Other miracles, such as weeping statues, are even easier to rig. In fact, charlatans have pulled off hoaxes at least since the sixteenth century, when a Portuguese nun faked stigmata by sampling painting wounds on her hands and feet. In 1986, a Montreal man named Jean-Guy Beauregard drew thousands of visitors when he reported that his statue of the Virgin Mary and other icons were crying tears—and in some cases blood. But after the Canadian Broadcasting Corp. borrowed the statue and took it to a laboratory, investigators discovered a mixture of pork and beef fat and Beauregard's own blood on the plaster face. When the room warmed, the fat liquefied and the "blood" dripped.[3]

Other "miracles" are sometimes optical illusions. Three years ago thousands of people mobbed a church in Colfax, California, to see an image on the wall purportedly of the Virgin Mary, which later turned out to be sunlight bouncing off a new lighting fixture.[4]

COUNTERFEIT OR TRUE MIRACLES?

There is no question that Satan will try to distract or deceive people by the use of false teachers, false prophets, and even false apostles. As incredible as it seems, some of these people will have the ability to manifest legitimate (not using trickery) supernatural signs and wonders, and those who are spiritually naïve will be impressed by their spiritual powers. These evidences of supernatural power exhibited by non-Christians are called "counterfeit miracles, signs and wonders" (2 Thess. 2:9). Paul may have been thinking of counterfeit miracles when he warned that the "Spirit clearly says that in later times some will abandon the faith and follow deceiving spirits and things taught by demons" (1 Tim. 4:1). From Scripture we understand that if a spiritual manifestation happens through the life of a person who is involved in the occult, the manifestation is not from God; it is from Satan. Some people are so impressed by a deceptive or demonically inspired sign and wonder or by the charisma of a false teacher that they will decide to follow a false god that appears to be very real.

By contrast, some have made the mistake of thinking that all signs, wonders, and manifestations are not from God, or they at least suspect them to be phony. It is easy to understand why persons who have been set up or deceived by religious scam artists would not trust a person who claims to have a ministry in which healing or miracles occur. It will take time to overcome the harm they have experienced.

We must use discernment to determine the true from the false, and we should not automatically think that miraculous manifestations are satanic deception or psychological manipulation. God used Moses to perform signs and wonders before Pharaoh when he was demanding the release of the Israelites from Egyptian captivity. Moses' staff was thrown to the ground, and it became a snake. (See Exodus 7:10.) Moses held his hand and staff over the water of the Nile and the water became blood. Moses' staff was held "over the streams and canals and ponds, and… frogs came up and covered the land" (Exod. 8:5–6). It is interesting, however, that the Bible says, "The Egyptian magicians also did the same things by their secret arts" (Exod. 7:11, 22; 8:7). To a point, they had the ability to duplicate miraculous manifestations, but eventually their ability to perform these counterfeit miracles was curtailed. We must remember that Satan has a limited amount of the supernatural power necessary to manifest signs and wonders, and his supernatural ability always falls short of God's miraculous power.

Paul told the Thessalonians that the Antichrist's works "will be in accordance with the work of Satan displayed in all kinds of counterfeit miracles, signs and wonders, and in every sort of evil that deceives those who are perishing" (2 Thess. 2:9–10). Yet Paul also wrote to the Corinthian church and described miracles, signs and wonders, and spiritual gifts that are to operate within the body of Christ. Satan will try to duplicate God's supernatural gifts as long as he can—until his end. He is the master counterfeiter, so we should not be surprised when we see or hear of someone who we know is not a Christian demonstrating some sort of supernatural manifestation.

Scripture clearly says that counterfeiting will occur, but that should not make us doubt God's acts of power through individuals in his church. We will see more abuse by the enemy's agents and misunderstanding of God's true gifts as we enter the twenty-first century. However, we can never let immaturity, false motives, or people's outright attempts to deceive prevent us from believing that God's supernatural gifts are for today and are part of His strategy for reaching this lost and dying world.

All miraculous manifestations are not of God. They may be from the enemy of our souls, they may be a manipulation of events that a selfish person has conjured up, or they may be an unwise handling of God's supernatural gifts by an immature Christian. In his book *Surprised by the Power of the Spirit*, Jack Deere comes to these conclusions about spiritual abuses:

> The presence of abuses and even impurity in Christian groups where miracles occur does not prove that miracles are not from God, any more than they did at Corinth. Second, the presence of doctrinal error in Christian groups where miracles occur does not prove the miracles are invalid, any more than it did in the Galatian churches. Third, miracles neither confirm nor support the distinctive doctrines or practices of individual churches or Christian groups. The miracles at Galatia did not support the heretical teaching there any more than the gift of miracles at Corinth supported their abuse of the Lord's Supper. According to Scripture, there is only one message that New Testament miracles support or confirm, and that is the gospel message concerning the person and work of Jesus Christ.[5]

Throughout the ages, God has consistently used signs and wonders and miracles to help His children and to demonstrate His power. Miracles happen because we have an amazing creative, merciful, and loving God who wants to make His power or Himself known to human- kind.

Corrie Ten Boom told the story of one such miracle:

> When rebels advanced on a school where two hundred children of missionaries lived, they planned to kill both children and teachers. In the school they knew of the danger and therefore went to prayer. Their only protection was a fence and a couple of soldiers, while the enemy, who came closer and closer, amounted to several hundred. When the rebels were close by, suddenly something happened: they turned around and ran away! The next day the same thing happened and again on the third

day. One of the rebels was wounded and was brought to the mission hospital. When the doctor was busy dressing his wounds, he asked him: "Why did you not break into the school as you planned?" "We could not do it. We saw hundreds of soldiers in white uniforms and we became scared." In Africa soldiers never wear white uniforms, so it must have been angels![6]

Corrie's story reminds us of an event in the apostle Peter's life. Peter was kept in prison, but the church was earnestly praying to God for him. The night before Herod was to bring him to trial, Peter was sleeping between two soldiers, bound with two chains, and sentries stood guard at the entrance. Suddenly an angel of the Lord appeared and a light shone in the cell. He struck Peter on the side and woke him up. "Quick, get up!" he said, and the chains fell off Peter's wrists:

> Then the angel said to him, "Put on your clothes and sandals." And Peter did so. "Wrap your cloak around you and follow me," the angel told him. Peter followed him out of the prison, but he had no idea that what the angel was doing was really happening; he thought he was seeing a vision. They passed the first and second guards and came to the iron gate leading to the city. It opened for them by itself, and they went through it. When they had walked the length of one street, suddenly the angel left him.
>
> —ACTS 12:8–10

Miracles, signs and wonders, and legitimate supernatural events do happen, but not all miracles are from God. Jack Deere writes:

> It is undeniable that there are significant abuses within some groups that believe in and practice the gifts of the Spirit. I have witnessed emotionalism, exaggerations, elitism, prophetic words used in a controlling and

manipulative way, and a lack of scriptural foundation in various meetings and movements. I would not say, however, that this is true of the majority of groups that practice the gifts of the Spirit. And I find that the leaders I know personally among these movements are quick to correct these excesses and abuses.[7]

It is not uncommon for unusual and perhaps controversial manifestations to be a part of people's reactions to God's presence. In times of great revival there have always been misunderstandings about manifestations, excesses, unwise decisions, and even people who fake a manifestation they see in another person, thinking they will receive some attention for their activity.

Jonathan Edwards was a tremendous eighteenth-century pastor who witnessed many unusual manifestations in his services and was concerned enough to discuss this topic in several of his writings. One point he continually made was that care should be taken not to say that a great move of God is occurring when one sees only manifestations. He rightly felt that the fruit in the person's life and the good effect on the community was the critical proof that God had done a work. In *The Distinguishing Marks of a Work of the Spirit of God*, he said:

> A work is not to be judged by any effects on the bodies of men, such as tears, trembling, groans, loud outcries, agonies of body, or the failing of bodily strength.... It is no argument that a work is not the Spirit of God that some who are the subjects of it have been in kind of ecstasy, wherein they have been carried beyond themselves, and have had their minds transported into a train of strong and pleasing.... visions, as though they were rapt up even to heaven, and there saw glorious sights. I have been acquainted with some such instances, and I see no need of bringing in the help of the devil into the account that we give of these things.[8]

John Wesley wrote of his close friend George Whitefield on July 7, 1739:

> I had an opportunity to talk with him of those outward signs, which had so often accompanied the inward work of God. I found his objections were chiefly grounded on gross misrepresentations of matter of fact. But the next day he had an opportunity of informing himself better: for no sooner had he begun (in the application of his sermon) to invite all sinners to believe in Christ, than four persons sank down close to him, almost in the same moment. One of them lay without either sense or motion; a second trembled exceeding; the third had strong convulsions all over his body, but made no noise, unless by groans; the fourth, equally convulsed, called upon God, with strong cries and tears. From this time I trust, we shall all suffer God to carry on His own work in the way that pleaseth Him.[9]

In his book *The Life and Travels of George Whitefield, M.A.*, James Patterson Gledstone writes:

> He had not spoken long before he perceived numbers melting; as he preceded the influence increased, till at last, both in the morning and afternoon, thousands cried out, so that they almost drowned his voice. "Oh what strong crying and tears," he says, "were shed and poured forth after the dear Lord Jesus! Some fainted, and when they had gotten a little strength, they would hear and faint again. Others cried out in a manner almost as if they were in the sharpest agonies of death. And after I had finished my last discourse, I myself was so overpowered with a sense of God's love, that it almost took away my life." The next day, at Fog's Manor, where Blair was minister, the congregation was as large as that at Nottingham, and as great, Whitefield says, "if not greater, commotion was in the hearts of the people. Look where

I would, most were drowned in tears. The word was sharper than a two-edged sword, and their bitter cries and groans were enough to pierce the hardest heart. Oh, what different visages were then to be seen! Some were struck pale as death, others were wringing their hands, others lying on the ground, others sinking into the arms of their friends, and most lifting up their eyes toward heaven, and crying out to God for mercy!"[10]

On numerous occasions, John Wesley himself witnessed manifestations during his preaching. He writes in his journal:

[July 19, 1757:] I preached in a ground adjoining to the house. Toward the conclusion of my sermon, the person with whom I lodged was much offended at one who sunk down and cried aloud for mercy. Herself drooped down next, and cried as loud as her, so did several others quickly after. When prayer was made for them, one was presently filled with peace and joy in believing.[11]

Saturday, June 14, 1759: Mr. Berridge, being ill, desired me to exhort a few people in his house, which the Lord enabled me to do with such ease and power that I was quite amazed. The next morning, at seven, his servant, Caleb Price, spoke to about two hundred people. The Lord was wonderfully present, more than twenty persons feeling the arrows of conviction. Several fell to the ground, some of whom seemed dead, others in the agonies of death, the violence of their bodily convulsions exceeding all description. There was such great crying and agonizing in prayer, mixed with deep and deadly groans on every side....A child, seven years old, sees many visions and astonishes the neighbors with her innocent, awful manner of declaring them....Some of those who were here pricked to the heart were affected in an astonishing manner. The first man I saw wounded would have dropped, but others, catching him in their arms, did, indeed, prop him up, but were so far from keeping still that he caused all of them to totter and tremble. His own shaking exceeded that of a cloth in the wind. It seemed as if the Lord came upon him like a giant, taking him by the neck and shaking all his bones in pieces.... Another roared and screamed in a more dreadful agony than ever I heard before.... Some continued long as if they were dead, but with a calm sweetness in their looks.[12]

Monday, August 6 1759:... I talked largely with Ann Thorn and two others, who had been several times in trances. What they all agreed in was: (1) that when they went away, as they termed it, it was always at the time they were fullest of the love of God; (2) that it came upon them in a moment, without previous notice, and took away all their sense and strength; (3) that there were some exceptions, but in general, from that moment they were in another world, knowing nothing of what was done or said by all that were around about them.... I have generally observed more or less of these outward symptoms to attend the beginning of a general work of God. So it was in New England, Scotland, Holland, Ireland, and many parts of England; but after a time, they gradually decrease, and the work goes on more quietly and silently.[13]

Charles Finney experienced some of the same kinds of manifestations in his ministry. He writes in his memoirs:

[in Adams, New York, in 1822:] Before the week was out I learned that some, when they would attempt to observe this season of prayer, would lose all of their strength and be unable to rise to their feet, or even stand upon their knees in their closets.[14]

[In Antwerp, New York,] The congregation began to fall from their seats in every direction, and cried for mercy.

If I had a sword in each hand, I could not have cut them off their seats as fast as they fell.[15]

As Jonathon Edwards experienced tremendous revival, he was also concerned that biblical guidelines be given to the manifestations that occurred. Edwards turned to Scripture and found five clear indications of a work of the Spirit of God. He felt that these features always mark genuine revival.

1. Acknowledgement of Christ

John wrote, "This is how you can recognize the Spirit of God: Every spirit that acknowledges that Jesus Christ has come in the flesh is from God, but every spirit that does not acknowledge Jesus is not from God. This is the spirit of the antichrist, which you have heard is coming and even now is already in the world" (1 John 4:2–3).

2. Attack on Satan's kingdom

"You, dear children, are from God and have overcome them, because the one who is in you is greater than the one who is in the world. They are from the world and therefore speak from the viewpoint of the world, and the world listens to them" (1 John 4:4–5).

False teachers who lived during John's day tried to infiltrate the young churches with a distorted version of conversion and the Christian life. In contrast to the kingdom of Christ there is a satanic "world system."

True revival always deals seriously with sin, focusing the attention on holiness and God's kingdom. Those affected by the Spirit of God typically show a strong distaste for anything corrupt, especially chasing after pleasure, applause, and commercial profit from the ministry.

3. Regard for Scripture

"We are from God, and whoever knows God listens to us; but whoever is not from God does not listen to us" (1 John 4:6). God used the apostles to complete the canon of Scripture that now stands as His final deposit of truth. Just as the Bible was given by the Spirit, so does the Spirit continue to draw men, women, and children to its pages. True revival does not cause people to hunger after new revelations while their Bibles remain unopened. True revival leads people to delight in God's Word. Edwards said, "The devil has ever shewn a mortal spite and hatred toward that holy book, the Bible: he has done all that has been in his power to extinguish that light, and to draw men off from it: he knows that `tis that light by which his kingdom of darkness is to be overthrown."[16]

4. Commitment to truth

"This is how we recognize the Spirit of truth and the spirit of falsehood" (1 John 4:6). We know that the devil is a liar and that his kingdom is darkness, "but everything exposed by the light becomes visible" (Eph. 5:13). In genuine revival, the Spirit leads people to the truth, and they become convinced of the Bible's truthfulness. This commitment to truth should be mirrored in the teaching and conduct of Christian leadership as well. Paul recognized that his ministry was a gift and that he himself was not the source of its life-changing power; God was. In contrast to those who built their ministries on the strength of their human talents, he wrote, "We have renounced secret and shameful ways; we do not use deception, nor do we distort the word of God. On the contrary, by setting forth the truth plainly we commend ourselves to every man's conscience in the sight of God" (2 Cor. 4:2).

5. Love for God and others

"Dear friends, let us love one another, for love comes from God. Everyone who loves has been born of God and knows God. Whoever does not love does not know God, because God is love.... And he has given us this command: Whoever loves God must also love his brother" (1 John 4:7–8, 21).

Scripture presents a clear picture of true love: Jesus giving His life for ours on the cross of Calvary. "Greater love has no one than this, that he lay down his life for his friends" (John 15:13). When Jesus told his disciples, "If you love me, you will obey what I command" (John 14:15), He inseparably linked love for Himself with a lifestyle of obedience to His words and, indeed, the whole Word of God. In scriptural terms, there is simply no love without obedience nor obedience without truth.[17]

ORDER IN THE CHURCH

Recently I received a telephone call from a pastor telling me that one of his church leaders had informed him that he had a "word from the Lord" saying that the pastor was to leave the church. Needless to say, the pastor became alarmed and for a few days was confused about this so-called personal prophecy. Neither the pastor nor the congregation in general had any indication that the Lord wanted him to leave the church. In fact, the church had grown substantially over the years, and it was having a good impact on the community for God's kingdom.

The church leader felt that the church was not doing some things that he thought were important, and, while praying he felt impressed that the church needed a new pastor. He then spoke to a few people who had the same opinion. They began getting together for discussion and prayer about the situation and together sensed that their feelings were God's will. As a result, they gave the pastor what they defined as a "personal prophecy."

The pastor met with his church board, and they unanimously agreed that the person was being disloyal and had not heard from God concerning the situation. The board promptly confronted the man who gave the prophecy and asked him to resign from his leadership position unless he changed his opinion. The person and the small group of people with whom he met left the church, and not surprisingly the people of the congregation have felt a greater sense of unity since they left.

Personal prophecy is something of which we need to be cautious. Does God use personal prophecy? Yes. (You will read an amazing example of one in the next chapter.) However, it must be biblical, must bear witness to what God has been speaking to us about, and must have the blessing of the spiritual leaders. (See Acts 13:1–5, 10–14.) A great deal of confusion and harm can come to a person's life or, as in the situation mentioned above, the whole church, when people are allowed to give what they call personal prophecies—without scrutiny.

In Paul's description of the spiritual gifts, he tells us that he does not want us to "be ignorant" (1 Cor. 12:1). We are to know about them and to know that there is a proper way to use them. Earlier, in chapter 6, we discussed the gifts and the fact that every member has at least one gift. It is also important to understand how to properly use the gifts. We can divide Paul's teaching on this subject into three principles: the principle of individual importance (1 Cor. 12), the principle of love (1 Cor. 13), and the principle of order (1 Cor. 14).

THE PRINCIPLE OF INDIVIDUAL IMPORTANCE (1 CORINTHIANS 12)

Every member of the body of Christ has at least one spiritual gift, and every member is important. It is God's plan for the church to operate as a unit just as our physical bodies operate as a unit. We need our eyes, arms, hearts, kidneys, and so on to function in a healthy manner; and the body of Christ needs every person and every gift in order to have maximum impact on a community.

> The body is a unit, though it is made up of many parts;
> and though all its parts are many, they form one body. So
> it is with Christ. For we were all baptized by one Spirit
> into one body—whether Jews or Greeks, slave or free—
> and we were all given the one Spirit to drink.
> —1 CORINTHIANS 12:12–13

We are part of a worldwide body of believers in Jesus Christ, and we are to depend on one another. In his commentary on Corinthians, William Barclay writes:

> 1. We ought to realize that we need each other. There can be no such thing as isolation in the Church. Far too often people in the Church become so engrossed in the bit of the work that they are doing and so convinced of its supreme importance that they neglect or even criticize others who have chosen to do other work. If the Church is to be a healthy body, we need the work that everyone can do.

> 2. We ought to respect each other. In the body there is no question of relative importance. If any limb or any organ ceases to function, the whole body is thrown out of gear. It is so with the Church. "All service ranks the same with God." Whenever we begin to think about our own importance in the Christian Church, the possibility of real Christian work is gone.

> 3. We ought to sympathize with each other. If any one part of the body is affected, all the others suffer in sympathy because they cannot help it. The Church is a whole. The person who cannot see beyond his or her own organization, the person who cannot see beyond his or her congregation, worse still, the person who cannot see beyond his or her own family circle, has not even begun to grasp the real unity of the Church.[18]

THE PRINCIPLE OF LOVE
(1 CORINTHIANS 13)

Our motivation for utilizing the gifts God has given us should always be love. We never use a God-given gift out of selfishness, pride, one-upmanship, or arrogance. We operate in the gifts of the Spirit out of our love for God, His body (other Christians), and the world we are called to reach for His glory. We are motivated by love; therefore, we are intensely interested in the well-being of the people we serve as we use our God-given spiritual gifts. Paul said, "Love never fails. But where there are prophecies, they will cease; where there are tongues, they will be stilled; where there is knowledge, it will pass away. For we know in part and we prophesy in part, but when perfection comes, the imperfect disappears.... And now these three remain: faith, hope and love. But the greatest of these is love" (1 Cor. 13:8–10, 13).

If people have dynamic gifts and charismatic abilities but do not demonstrate God's love in what they do and say, do not pay any attention to them. God's gifts and God's love work hand in hand.

God's love motivates us to minister to people in God's ways. We must sincerely care, have compassion, and want to help people because God does. More important than the gift we use is how we demonstrate the love of God toward others. Augustine said, "What does love look like? It has the hands to help others. It has the feet to hasten to the poor and needy. It has the eyes to see misery and want. It has the ears to hear the sighs and sorrows of men. That is what love looks like."[19]

THE PRINCIPLE OF ORDER
(1 CORINTHIANS 14)

We must be sensitive to using the gifts of the Spirit at the proper time. There are three guidelines we should understand. First, all of the gifts are important to the well-being of the church. Second, everyone in the body is important and has gifts given by the Holy Spirit. Third, the number of times certain gifts (tongues and prophecy) are to be used in a service is limited.

People can become selfish, saying, "I want to use my gift" or "My gift is more important than their gifts." This is not a loving or cooperative attitude. Theologian Gordon Fee writes, "Each one has something to contribute, and everything must be done to edify. This is followed by guidelines, first for tongues and interpretation (1 Cor. 14:27–28) and then for prophecy and discernment (vv. 29–31). Christian inspiration is not out of control, for God Himself is not like that; and this holds for all the congregations of the saints."[20]

Paul tells the church that every time a message in tongues is given in a church service, there must be an interpretation (1 Cor. 14:27–28). The interpretation can either be given by someone else in the congregation or by the person giving the message. Paul instructs the church on how many prophecies should be given during a church service (v. 29). And he teaches that the prophecy should be weighed carefully and judged to determine whether it is from God or not. "God is a God of peace, not disorder" (1 Cor. 14:33), and "everything should be done in a fitting and orderly way" (1 Cor. 14:40).

How to Recognize False Manifestations or False Teachers

Is the service handled in a biblical way?

Is the Bible used as the final authority for all that is communicated, and is it used to confirm all that happens in the service? As you participate in the worship and observe the preaching, what is your overall impression of the service? Do you feel that everything that has occurred can be supported by Scripture? This is critical, because the Bible must be believed and obeyed as the final authority in all things that pertain to life and godliness. (See Matthew 5:17–19; John 14:21; 15:10; 2 Timothy 3:15–16; 2 Peter 1:3.) God does not need anyone's human attempt to manipulate a miracle. God never operates in dishonesty. Charles Spurgeon said, "The Holy Spirit will never set His seal to falsehood. Never! If what you preach is not the truth, God will not own it. If we do not speak clear doctrine with plainness of speech, the Holy Spirit will not put his signature to our empty prating."[21]

The Scriptures must be used in the church as the final authority in all matters for teaching, reproof, correction, doctrine, and instruction in righteous living. (See 2 Timothy 3:16–17.) If manifestations are occurring and there is no biblical support, instruction, or resulting biblical fruit, then you must be cautious or reject the experience as not being from God. Miracles can be counterfeited, so we must put our trust in Christ through His Word. The Bible is a supernatural book given to us by our supernatural God to understand the true from the false, the real from the unreal, and legitimate miracles from counterfeit miracles.

Is the leader a Christian?

In his book Exploring the Future, John Phillips writes:

> Few people realize it, but occultism is at the root of Mormonism, one of the world's fastest-growing religious cults. The cult's leaders know the truth; the fact that Joseph Smith and other prominent founding fathers of Mormonism had recourse to the spirit world is too well documented to be denied."[22]

The late Walter Martin, who was probably as well versed in Mormon history and doctrine as anyone in this country, has exposed and documented the truth in *The Maze of Mormonism*. Martin:

> …told us, for instance, that Joseph Smith was an occultist who used a special "peepstone" to help translate his Bible. Wilford Woodruff, one of the early presidents of the Mormon cult, talked openly of his occult experiences. He claimed to have received visits from Joseph Smith, Brigham Young, and Heber C. Kimball on various occasions. These founders of Mormonism gave heed to "doctrines of demons." Paul warned of such and indicated that their teachings would be a feature of the last days. The fact that Mormonism puts on a respectable front for

the public consumption does not alter its murky past. Its antibiblical doctrines confirm the cult's source of inspiration. Nor do the present leaders of Mormonism repudiate the movement's founders. On the contrary, they glorify them and present carefully edited versions of their history to the public for mass consumption.[23]

There is always the possibility that another type of Joseph Smith could rise up and deceive many. Charismatic leaders have periodically done this throughout history. They might package their teaching from verses in the Bible and even appear to have some kind of spiritual authority. We must ask ourselves, however, does this person have a saving knowledge of the resurrected Lord, Jesus Christ? And is all that he or she teaches supported by Scripture?

We must also be aware that within churches there may be many who are not right with God or do not know God. Jesus Christ warned that not everyone who professes Him is a true believer. (See Matthew 7:21.) Besides ministers, this could include teachers, writers of "Christian" books, missionaries, evangelists, deacons, or church leaders. Commentator Donald Stamps writes:

> These impostors attain a place of influence in the church in two ways: (a) Some false teachers/preachers begin their ministry in sincerity, truth, purity, and genuine faith in Christ, then because of their pride and their own immoral desires, personal commitment and love to Christ gradually die; consequently, they are severed from the kingdom of God (see 1 Corinthians 6:9–10; Galatians 5:19–21; Ephesians 5:5–6) and become instruments of Satan while disguising themselves as ministers of righteousness, (2 Corinthians 11:15); (b) Other false teachers/preachers are never genuine believers in Christ; Satan has planted them within the church from the very beginning of their ministry (see Matthew 13:24–28,

36–43), using their ability and charisma and aiding in their success; his strategy is to place them in influential positions so that they can undermine the genuine work of Christ; if they are discovered or exposed, Satan knows that great damage will come to the gospel and that the name of Christ will be put to open shame.[24]

Do the leader and any accompanying miracles demonstrate God's fruit?

A false teacher will often purposefully omit portions of God's Word and as a result produce converts who are not committed to the whole Bible. The leader's life may not demonstrate a sincere devotion to God. It is also helpful to know whether a leader has financial responsibility. If godly fruit is not part of a person's life or ministry, we can be sure that person is not of God.

Does your spirit bear witness during the event?

Even though our feelings can be wrong about an individual or experience, it is important to listen to our emotions. How do we feel about what the person is preaching? Do we feel uneasy? Do we find ourselves wondering about the person's motives or if what we are seeing is a manipulation of events or of people's minds? These feelings could be the Holy Spirit warning or cautioning us. However, it is important that we justify our feelings with Scripture. Not all of our feelings are spiritual, and we could be having a personality conflict or a reaction to an opinion that is different than ours—or we could just be having a bad day.

We know that in spite of all that we can do to evaluate a person's life and message, there will still be false teachers within the churches who, with the help of Satan, remain undetected until God determines to expose them for what they are.[25]

Remember that the end result of everything we do is to lift up Jesus Christ. Our goal in preaching, our goal in a worship service, and our goal with people is that those to whom we minister completely surrender their lives to Jesus. Our focus should not be on the manifestation but on Jesus Christ. He is the author and finisher of our faith. He is the resurrected Lord who will one day come and take us to heaven for eternity. Manifestations are a natural part of the church of Jesus Christ, and they will be until the end.

Chapter 9

THE BENEFITS:
BOLDNESS AND STRENGTH

T HE PROPHETIC UTTERANCE kept repeating the word
Para, with instructions for Daniel Berg and Gunnar
Vingren to go there and begin preaching. But where
was Para?

Daniel Berg immigrated from Sweden to the United States
in 1902 with Gunnar Vingren following in 1903. From the
time they first gazed at the Ellis Island immigration process-
ing facility, they wondered where life would take them in this
new land of opportunity. At twenty-four and eighteen years
of age respectively, they could not have anticipated the creative future that God had prepared for them. Both were sol-
idly committed Christians, and together they prayed that God
would accomplish His will in their lives.

Gunnar became the pastor of a small Baptist church in South
Bend, Indiana, where Daniel also became involved. It was at a
Bible study there that the two men heard a prophetic utterance
that repeated the word *Para*. The prophecy instructed both
Gunnar and Daniel to go to this location and begin a work for
God's kingdom.[1] Curious about this possible change in events,
they went to the South Bend Public Library and searched the
World Almanac for Para with no success. Finally, the librarian
directed them to the World Atlas. Para was a state located in
the northeast part of Brazil.

Within months Gunnar and Daniel made plans to go to

Brazil. They felt that the Lord had given them specific instructions to leave on November 5, 1910, from New York. Gunnar had been able to save ninety dollars for travel costs. However, when he heard about a Pastor Durham who needed finances for his Pentecostal newspaper, he gave the money to that need. Gunnar's congregation gave them enough money to go to Chicago, where they were invited to speak in a church service for Pastor B. M. Johnson. The pastor asked his congregation if anyone would like to help Gunnar and Daniel with their mission to Brazil. Many responded to the need of the two young missionaries. However, not until later, when checking their pockets, did they count four times the amount of money they had given away.

Gunnar and Daniel were disappointed when they arrived in New York and there was no ship leaving on November 5 for Brazil. After searching, they found the *Clement*, a steamer that had been delayed because of repairs but to their amazement was now ready to leave on November 5. Because of a New York harbor strike, the men had to leave their trunks. Fourteen days later they were in Brazil.

Upon arriving in the country that they felt the Lord had brought them to, Gunnar and Daniel did not know where to start or what to do. While sitting on a park bench praying for guidance, they met a Methodist missionary who introduced them to a local pastor. They were given permission to begin a prayer meeting in his church, and as a result, many people were baptized in the Holy Spirit. Out of that group the Apostolic Faith Mission began, and on June 11, 1918, they registered their church work with the government as the Assemblies of God.

From these humble beginnings, the message of salvation and the baptism in the Holy Spirit spread like a wildfire. From friend to friend, village-to-village, city-to-city, and state-to-state, their message exploded throughout Brazil. What had begun in a small prayer meeting in South Bend, Indiana, had now become reality in thousands of people's lives. In Rio fifty years later, in 1961, approximately forty thousand people attended the "half-century" celebration of the Pentecostal message coming to Brazil. In July 1967 believers could be found all over the country and were having the world's largest gatherings of Pentecostals. By 1970 many millions of people in Brazil claimed to be Pentecostal. Today there are more than twenty million Pentecostals in that nation including eighteen million members in the Assemblies of God alone. We can only guess the number of Pentecostals who are a part of the other church fellowships and denominational groups.

In September of 1997 I visited Brazil and attended a prayer meeting of hundreds of thousands of believers. President Fernando Henriguo greeted the crowd, and other government officials were in attendance. Television cameras throughout the massive crowd recorded what was happening in these people's lives. As I looked at the crowd and thought about how to address them, I was amazed at God's faithfulness. Eighty-six years earlier two young Swedish men named Daniel Berg and Gunnar Vingren had boldly taken a great faith risk. Something happened in their hearts that persuaded them to go to a place of which they had never heard to bring the precious gospel of Jesus Christ and the message of the baptism in the Holy Spirit. They had most likely had doubts, experienced numerous hardships, and met many people who wondered about the logic of what they were doing. However, today there is no doubt of God's strategy there. Looking back over the twentieth century, the Christian growth in Brazil has proven that Daniel and Gunnar were prompted by the Holy Spirit.

The story of Daniel and Gunnar is not an unusual one in the history books of the Christian faith. Luke records, "Paul had a vision of a man of Macedonia standing and begging him, 'Come over to Macedonia and help us.' After Paul had seen the vision, we got ready at once to leave for Macedonia, concluding that God had called us to preach the gospel to them" (Acts

16:9–10). Paul demonstrated a unique boldness and courage to obey all that God had instructed him to do regardless of the hardships.

The power (Acts 1:8) that people receive when they are baptized in the Holy Spirit enables them to be greater witnesses for Christ. They have a longing to tell others about Jesus and teach all that He commanded. Even if their personalities are timid, they have a unique confidence to speak to others about Jesus.

The early church was known for their amazing tenacity, and their hearts were stirred with passion to take the message of Christ to their world despite the threat of persecution. Jesus had predicted this would happen when He said, "You will receive power when the Holy Spirit comes on you; and you will be my witnesses" (Acts 1:8). The two main clauses in this verse, "You will receive power" and "you will be my witnesses," are interrelated. "Receiving" and "being" work hand in hand. After the Holy Spirit came on them, they would tell what they had seen, heard, and experienced. Beginning in Jerusalem they would carry their witness through "Judea and Samaria and unto the uttermost part of the earth." Theologian Stanley Horton has said, "This program for witnessing also gives us a virtual table of contents for the Book of Acts."[2]

Peter and John were put in jail because they refused to stop speaking about Jesus. (See Acts 4:18.) In fact, when they were released, they gathered with many believers and loudly prayed. "'Now, Lord, consider their threats and enable your servants to speak your word with great boldness. Stretch out your hand to heal and perform miraculous signs and wonders through the name of your holy servant Jesus.' After they prayed, the place where they were meeting was shaken. And they were all filled with the Holy Spirit and spoke the word of God boldly" (Acts 4:29–31).

Late pastor, writer, and theologian Martyn Lloyd-Jones wrote:

You cannot read the New Testament accounts of the people to whom the Spirit came, these people whom He fell, or who received as the Galatian Christians and all these others had done, without realizing that the result was that their whole spirit was kindled. The Lord Jesus Christ became real to them in a way that He had never been before. The Lord Jesus Christ manifested Himself to them spiritually, and the result was a great love for Christ, shed abroad in their hearts by the Holy Spirit.

Now this, surely, is something which should cause us to pause for a moment and meditate very deeply and very seriously. This is an experience, as I understand this teaching, which is the birthright of every Christian. "For the promise," says the apostle Peter, "is unto you"—and not only to you but—"to your children, and to all that are afar off" (Acts 2:39, KJV). It is not confined just to these people on the Day of Pentecost but is offered to and promised to all Christian people. And in its essence it means that we are conscious of the incoming, as it were, of the Spirit of God and are given a sense of the glory of God and the reality of His being, the reality of the Lord Jesus Christ, and we love Him.... And that, as you read these accounts, is the invariable result of this baptism of the Holy Spirit. Furthermore, you will find that this is something to which the saints of the centuries have testified. Everybody remembers the story of how this happened to John Wesley in Aldersgate Street in London in 1738, but many people have never heard of it as it happened in a still more striking manner to George Whitefield before that. We have heard of it in the case of Moody, walking down the street in New York City one afternoon, when suddenly he became aware of the glory of God in such an overwhelming manner that he felt that even his strong body was on the point of being crushed, and he held up his hands and asked God to stop. It is true of Finney and Jonathan Edwards and David Brainerd. It is something to which many ordinary Christians, whose names we do not know, have testified and for which they have thanked God: this sense of the glory of God; the reality of the Lord; this love toward Him; this indescribable experience of these things.[3]

John Fletcher said, "Every Christian should have his Pentecost."[4]

Throughout the last two thousand years, the church of Jesus Christ has repeatedly demonstrated supernatural courage. In our humanness we are not capable of conjuring up this kind of courage. We need the power that comes only from the infilling of the Holy Spirit. Although physical and mental strength is helpful, being filled with the Spirit provides much more than physical ability or mental discipline. It is more than "the power of positive thinking." It is not some mental or intellectual exercise that we develop through meditation. Nor is it acquired by receiving a theological degree. When we are baptized in the Holy Spirit, our lives are deeply and dynamically touched by God, and we become eager to do God's mighty works. Throughout the Book of Acts, we see this power manifested by Spirit-filled Christians exhibiting authority to drive out demonic spirits and heal the sick. The baptism in the Holy Spirit released God's power in believers' lives, and they gained a new confidence and boldness to speak out about the resurrected Christ. This happened then and it still happens today. G. Campbell Morgan said, "The nature of the power is evident. It is the coming of God to man for the accomplishment of a Divine purpose in this sacred partnership. Man is helpless apart from this immediate cooperation with God. God chooses to be helpless apart from cooperation with man."[5]

We need to understand at least three things about the Holy Spirit's power.

WE NEED GOD'S POWER

Perhaps more now than at any time in history, we need God's power and discernment. As we approach the time when the Antichrist will be revealed, Satan will do all he can to influence people to his cause and try to distract and deceive even the church. Jesus said, "For false Christs and false prophets will appear and perform great signs and miracles to deceive even the elect—if that were possible" (Matt. 24:24).

Although we enjoy much of what technology has provided, we must be cautious that we do not buy into all of its advancements. We will need God's wisdom and power to stand for our convictions and discern what is truly helpful to our Christian lives.

On a recent airplane trip, I sat next to a gentleman who was a computer expert. He was on his way to a large corporate headquarters to help a billion-dollar company understand the new opportunities coming in the world of the Internet, Web sites, virtual reality, and programming. I am somewhat illiterate concerning sophisticated computer language, but this executive explained situations and scenarios that concerned, even frightened me.

He talked about the pornography industry that has invaded the Internet and how there would soon be opportunity for people to act out their sexual fantasies through virtual reality. When I gave him my opinion that pornography was wrong and asked him what he thought about it, he disagreed with me that it was a moral problem and said, "Come on...it's only entertainment!" He talked about being able to communicate with people thousands of miles away in chat rooms and at the same time view them on a large monitor. He brought me up to date on how fast the computer industry is developing and said that anyone could do just about anything, buy anything, and experience anything in the privacy of his or her home or office. I understand and enjoy some of the positive aspects of computers and the Internet, but I could not help thinking about the people who will buy into this filth of what is offered and as a result greatly injure their lives and relationships. Sin has become sophisticated, and the ability to rationalize wrong behavior has become the norm of the day in which we live.

Life magazine reported:

> We are about to enter a millennium of miracles. If a person cuts off his hand while fixing a lawn mower, doctors will be able to grow him a new one. Houses and cars will be made of materials that can fix themselves when damaged. There will be a white powered food that is 90 percent protein and can be made to taste like almost anything.
>
> These predictions may sound bold, but in truth they're pretty conservative.... We do not know when, if ever, we will have robot slaves...time machines. But we do know that whatever miracles the next millennium holds, all will be wrought by the same genie: the computer.
>
> Computers, the electronic brains behind intelligent metals, miraculous foods and replacement organs, are growing smarter by the minute. According to Moore's Law (propounded by Gordon Moore, cofounder of Intel), they get twice as smart every 18 months. They are already 130,000 times smarter than when silicon chips were introduced in 1971. Paul Horn, senior vice president of research at IBM, says Moore's Law will apply for at least another fifteen years.
>
> ...As computer scientist Carl Feynman of Art Technology Group puts it, "We've discovered that the gray mush in our heads is probably not the best material for thinking." Computers will soon use their superior "thinking material" to make themselves even smarter. Humans and computers already design new generations of computers together; but, Horn says, as time goes by, people will be phased out of the process.[6]

The Bible tells us that Satan will empower a man during the seven-year period we call the Tribulation who will be able to create an "image" (not human) of the Antichrist. This image will be able to breathe, speak, and kill people who refuse to take the Antichrist's "mark" on their foreheads or right hand. (See Revelation 13:11–17.) Could this image be nothing more than a twenty-first-century technologically advanced machine that looks, thinks, and acts humanlike without any sense of moral restraint or conscience? This could very possibly be the case.

Recently in the news is the controversy over cloning human bodies for the purpose of harvesting body parts. Leaders of some nations have not shown much concern over the morality of cloning and have refused to sign an agreement saying that they would refrain from cloning humans. Technology and components for nuclear, biological, and chemical weapons have been obtained by countries that do not have much moral restraint in using them. Submarines and jet fighters are being sold to nations that will use them against the free world without a moment's hesitation if they see an advantage in it. As Daniel said concerning the last days, "Many will go here and there to increase knowledge" (Dan. 12:4). Knowledge will greatly increase throughout the world; however, moral restraint, a sense of rightness, and God's righteousness will decrease for non-Christians as we and they approach Armageddon.

Temptation is becoming more sophisticated and consistent, and the enemy of our souls is perhaps more aggressive than at any other time in history, because he is aware that the second coming of Christ is rapidly approaching. Therefore, we need a supernatural power that will enable us to stand in spite of the forces against us.

We also need supernatural intellectual understanding of the will and power of God. Since we often are unsure about how our Master desires for us to fulfill His will, we need supernatural spiritual power to combat Satan's constant temptations and distractions. When we are tempted to compromise our convictions, we need to be able to firmly and completely say no to the devil's devices and yes to the righteous will of God. We need the power of God to walk away from the affections of this world and keep our eyes clearly focused on a better world. And we need God's *dunamis* to accomplish the goal of reaching every village, tribe, and nation with the gospel of Jesus Christ.

The early church needed unique power to be a witness to a world that had not heard of Jesus Christ. The church of the twenty-first century needs God's power to complete the task. William Barclay explains:

> This power of the Spirit was going to make [the early church] Christ's witness. That witness was to operate in an ever-extending series of concentric circles, first in Jerusalem, then throughout Judea; then Samaria, the semi-Jewish state, would be a kind of bridge leading out into the heathen world; and finally this witness was to go out to the ends of the earth.[7]

The primary purpose of receiving the baptism in the Holy Spirit is "power" for service. The early church needed a supernatural power to pioneer the gospel of Jesus Christ to the world. Today's world is characterized by wars, rumors of wars, famines, earthquakes, moral decay, apathy, false Christs, and tremendous deceptions. (See Matthew 24, Mark 13, and Luke 21.) Stanley M. Horton says:

> The followers of Jesus must go out and spread the gospel to all nations in the midst of all these natural calamities and political upheavals. How would this be possible? They would receive power as a result of being filled with the Spirit. This would be their secret of success in the Church Age until its final consummation when Jesus returns. Of course, this puts a great responsibility to be Christ's witness on all who are filled with the Spirit.[8]

In our human strength, we cannot do it. The Father has given us the baptism in the Holy Spirit because He knows that we need a dynamite power within our beings to fight the enemy and accomplish great things for God's kingdom.

WHAT *DUNAMIS* IS

As Steve grew into a young man, he became hopelessly addicted to drugs. He had no concern for people or even for his own health. At sixteen Steve became more rebellious when his father unexpectedly died of a heart attack. After that, Steve's life was a rollercoaster ride with a death wish. He spent the rest of his teen years in and out of jail, in a fog of endless drug-induced highs and terrifying lows.

Through it all, Steve heard a voice within him that grew louder and louder, and he experimented with drugs, alcohol, and reckless living. This voice demanded that he use drugs to soothe the pain he felt, and it demanded that he steal from stores, friends, and his own family to finance his expensive habit.

Steve watched as one after another of his friends died. Manny was first—he was stabbed to death. Frankie died of an overdose. Toby died when he wrapped his car around a telephone pole. Sammy's life was snatched away when he hit a truck. Bobbie hanged himself. Steve thought about death, and the voice within him encouraged him to plan for it. He thought that Bobbie had taken the easy way out.

Steve's physical, mental, and emotional life was a mess. He was full of confusion and was physically dying. His body had had enough and was shutting down. During this time, he said, "I realized for the first time that this evil voice and power [inside of me] was 'the destroyer.' His intention all along was not to help me but to destroy me.

"I wanted to be free from his destruction, [but] all I could do was lay there and try to resist, knowing that my strength and resistance were failing fast."

During this time a young man visited Steve. He said, "Steve, I've come because you're hurting. I can't help you, but I know somebody who can. His name is Jesus, and he's here with us. He wants to help you!"

Steve was desperate. Death was near and the young man knew it. He encouraged Steve by explaining that Jesus would touch him if he would cry out to Him. "Just cry out the name, Jesus! Jesus!" he said.

Steve said, "The sound of that name again and again seemed to bring hope from nowhere." Steve looked at the ceiling above him and said, "Jesus, Jesus, Jesus, Jesus."

With that name, confusion and fear faded and a peace and warmth rushed throughout Steve's body. Steve surrendered his life to Jesus Christ. He said, "The power rushed in like a river and took command of everything. I kept crying out his name, louder and louder. The convulsions I was experiencing stopped. The evil presence vanished." Steve had been born again.

A few weeks after Steve's salvation experience, narcotics officers apprehended him on felony drug charges. His past had been forgiven by God, but he would have to pay for what he had done during his reckless years of drug abuse.

Steve was put in jail to await his court date. During those months, he focused on his relationship with the Lord. He was concerned about the possibility that he could go to prison for years because of his numerous crimes. Finally, the court date arrived, and Steve found himself before a judge whom he had seen many times.

Steve's heart pounded, and his thoughts rushed back and forth, fearful of what degree of sentence he would face that day. The judge said, "Steve Hill, this is against my better judgment, but I sentence you to Outreach Ministries of Alabama. If you do not successfully complete the program, you will spend years in the penitentiary."

Incredible! Steve could not believe it. Why did the judge give this kind of sentence? It was a miracle. After three months,

Steve transferred to Teen Challenge in Cape Girardeau, Missouri. Steve said, "In Teen Challenge, I learned to live out my professions of love and faith in Christ. I was water baptized, filled with the Holy Spirit, learned how to not just read but study the Bible, and I became disciplined in prayer."

Steve's life became balanced, and he became a tremendous witness for Christ and sensed a call to full-time ministry. God gave him a wonderful wife, and in 1992 Steve and Jeri went to Latin America as missionary evangelists. They also started churches in Colombia, Spain, and the former Soviet Union. Over two decades after his conversion experience, Steve and Jeri came to an Assemblies of God church in Brownsville, Florida, as visiting evangelists. On that Father's Day of 1995, something began that Steve or the church did not completely expect. What is now called the Brownsville Revival began.

Steve, who had once heard the destructive voice within him, now heard the Holy Spirit's healing voice encouraging him to tell the world about God's wonderful plan of salvation and deliverance. Steve said, "Drug addicts have been delivered, prostitutes off the streets have been saved, people have been healed, and hundreds of marriages have been restored."

On a recent visit to the church, I was overjoyed to see all kinds of people—rich, poor, and a variety of races and nationalities. People had come from all over the world to experience the revival. It is common to see teenagers with pierced noses, eyelids, lips, and tongues. Some have green, red, or blue hair. These kids come off the streets looking for answers and find "the Answer" soon after they begin attending church and hearing the gospel of Jesus Christ. Steve says, "After they become saved, we don't even need to mention their colored hair or taking out the earrings. The Holy Spirit reminds them about what is inappropriate in time and they respond to him. Lots of the young people you see that are 'cleaned up' used to have colored hair and pierced bodies." Steve finds a strength within and a never-ending passion to teach these people who are hungry for God. "As long as the people come," he says, "I will be here. This is the opportunity of a lifetime, and the opportunity of a lifetime must be seized during the lifetime of the opportunity."[9]

Steve's life is an example of how God gives power to live a righteous life. Jesus said, "You will receive power when the Holy Spirit comes on you; and you will *be* my witnesses" (Acts 1:8; emphasis added). The word *be* means not only outwardly to be a witness but also to be all that Christ intends us to be. This power gives us a supernatural boldness and courage born of the Spirit. With it we become effective and infective witnesses for Jesus Christ.

The empowered witness bears certain characteristics. William Barclay has written:

> Let us note certain things about this Christian witness.
>
> First, a witness is a man who says I know this is true. In a court of law a man cannot give in evidence a carried story; it must be his own personal experience. There was a time when John Bunyan was not quite sure. What worried him was that the Jews thought their religion the best: the Mohammedans thought theirs the best; what if Christianity were but a think-so too? A witness does not say, "I think so"; he says, "I know."
>
> Second, the real witness is not of words but of deeds. When Stanley had discovered Livingstone in Central Africa and had spent some time with him, he said, "If I had been with him any longer I would have been compelled to be a Christian and he never spoke to me about it at all." The witness of the man's life was irresistible.
>
> Third, in Greek the word for witness and the word for Martyr is the same (*martus*). A witness had to be ready to become a martyr. To be a witness means to be loyal no matter the cost.[10]

There have been more Christian martyrs in the twentieth century than in any century since the inception of the church. The church will be persecuted more and more until the second coming of Jesus. Certain parts of the world, such as China, the former republics of the Soviet Union, Iran, Iraq, and other parts of the Middle East, are hotbeds for Christian persecution. While we need to do everything we can to prevent persecution, it is nevertheless a fact that it will exist. The power that accompanies the filling with the Spirit will enable believers to be willing to give up anything for the cause of Christ—even their physical lives if necessary.

As we pointed out earlier, before Peter was baptized in the Holy Spirit, a servant girl frightened him. He denied the Lord and ran because she threatened to reveal that he had been one of Jesus' disciples. Just a few weeks later, however, Peter boldly stood before thousands and proclaimed the resurrected Christ. Peter was no longer afraid, because he had the power of the Holy Spirit within him.

We also gain dynamic power for living when we receive the baptism in the Holy Spirit. We obtain power to overcome our addictions, improve our marriage, control our bad temper, and resist temptation. If we are single, we can have the strength to live a celibate life until married. If we are married, we can be faithful to our spouse. We can be a witness to those who have intimidated us and we can forgive those who have hurt us. We can "be" a witness by the way we live. People are watching us to see if we will really live the way we say Christians should live. When they see us living a compassionate, righteous life, they will be attracted to the message of Christ.

WHY *DUNAMIS* IS GIVEN TO US

We need God's supernatural power to reach this lost world for Christ. Concerning the reason God gave the baptism of the Holy Spirit, G. Campbell Morgan said of the early church:

Persecution awaited them. All the forces that had been against their Master would oppose them. The doctrine of deliverance, which they were to announce, was revolutionary, and the powers that held men in slavery would array themselves to silence their voices and stop their progress. If they were to continue bearing witness to him through darkness as well as light, when the way was rough as well as when it was smooth, through the perils of popularity as well as through the dangers of ostracism, they needed some new power of the affection and the will, which should make their lives burn as a flame, and set their faces as flint.... This power is precisely what Jesus promised in the indwelling Spirit.[11]

There is a unique faith and courage that is part of the lives of those who have received the baptism in the Holy Spirit. In the face of persecution and even death, they continue the mission of telling others about Christ. In spite of the odds, they go on. Something within their being motivates them to trust God, walk by faith, reach the unreached, and go where others will not go. They are calculated risk takers. Jesus, in Matthew 24, stresses that the church of the last days cannot wait for ideal conditions before spreading the gospel to every nation. He said that this age would be distinguished by false prophets and false Christ's, great deception, wars, rumors of wars, famines, and earthquakes. In the thick of all this, the followers of Jesus Christ must go to the world without Christ. How could this be possible? They would receive a unique power, *dunamis*, as a result of being filled with the Spirit. This would be the driving force that would help the church achieve the goal of reaching a world that is under the control of Satan. Someone has said, "They cannot drive the world until they themselves are driven."[12] There is a sense of being driven to reach "one more" and go the extra mile with the work God has called them to.

POWER FOR YOU

If you are like me, you want all of the power of God you can get. You desire to be a witness. You yearn to have mastery over life-controlling problems. You are hungry for everything God has for you. This hunger is critical, because when God sees our pure hunger for more of Him, He will fill us.

God never plays games with us or tries to trick us. He is a wonderful, good, and generous God, who will give you this blessing when He sees your life of repentance and your hungry heart, and hears your sincere request. (See Luke 11:11–13.) Jesus said, "'If anyone is thirsty, let him come to me and drink. Whoever believes in me, as the Scripture has said, streams of living water will flow from within him.' By this he meant the Spirit, whom those who believed in him were later to receive" (John 7:37–39).

Whether a person is Spirit-filled or not, he or she needs to have a continual thirst for God. A body of water that does not have any inlets or outlets becomes like the Dead Sea. Spiritually, we are like that. If we do not have an intake from the Spirit and an outflow as a result of that intake, we will become stagnant in our Christian experience. Jesus was saying that if we will receive the infilling of the Spirit, He will empower us to be witnesses—the outflow will be effective. We become golden pipes through which the golden oil of the Spirit flows. I believe this is what Zechariah was referring to when he said, "What are these two olive branches beside the two gold pipes that pour out golden oil?" (Zech. 4:12). When the Holy Spirit flows through our lives, there is a supernatural power that this world does not understand.

Jack Hayford reminds us of three points concerning this power:

1. The Holy Spirit is the Person and the Power by which assistance and ability are given for serving, for

sharing the life and power of God's kingdom with others.

2. The Holy Spirit's power must be "received"; it is not an automatic experience. As surely as the Holy Spirit indwells each believer (see Romans 8:9), so surely will He fill and overflow (see John 7:37–39) each who receives the Holy Spirit in childlike faith.

3. When the Holy Spirit fills you, you will know it. Jesus said it and the disciples found it true (Acts 1:5; 2:1–4). Have you received the Holy Spirit? (See Acts 19:1–6.) You may, for the promise is as fully yours today as at any time in the past. (See Acts 2:38–39.)[13]

WHERE ARE YOU?

One of the great testimonies of what is happening around the world today is that Spirit-filled believers are evangelizing the world, touching multitudes, and as a result seeing lives change. God has given these people tremendous boldness. They are unashamed to live righteous Christian lives, and they are powerfully testifying of the new life that Jesus offers. The Christian life is not boring; it is exciting to walk by faith and see God answer prayer. It is invigorating to see people come to Christ because of your witness, and it is a wonderful feeling to know that the Holy Spirit is flowing through your life as you live for Christ. There are a lot of bored, apathetic, stuck Christians in the world today. Frankly, I do not understand this. Because when the Holy Spirit is moving through your life, there is a tremendous sense of excitement, and your Christian life seems fresh, not stale.

Are you hungry for more of God? Do you need more power to do what you feel He wants you to do? Is your Christian experience fresh and alive? Do you need boldness to stand against the enemy of your soul or tow witness to those around you? Please know this—God's power is for you. He wants your Christian life to be filled with His energy, and He desires to use you in ways that few understand.

Tell God that you are hungry for more. Ask Him to fill you with boldness and power. If you are not hungry, ask God to help you become hungry. We have all gone through dry spells in our Christian lives. During these times, we hold steady and ask God to give us a new hunger. Spurgeon said:

> Brothers, let us go in to get of God all that God will give us: let us set our heart upon this, that we mean to have by God's help all that the infinite goodness of God is ready to bestow. Let us not be satisfied with the sip that saves, but let us go on to the baptism which buries the flesh and raises us in the likeness of the risen Lord: even the baptism into the Holy Ghost and into fire which makes us spiritual and sets us all on flame with zeal for the glory of God and eagerness for usefulness by which that glory may be increased among the sons of men.[14]

If there has ever been a time when we need God's supernatural boldness and power, it is today. There has never been a day like the day in which we live. Evil seems more prevalent now than at any other time in history, and the enemy will do everything he can to stop the church from reaching more for Christ. But Satan's power is limited. He cannot stop Spirit-filled Christians from doing all that God has asked them to do. You can have this power. Your hungry heart and your request is all that God needs to see and hear.

Chapter 10

THE IMPACT:
WORLDWIDE OUTREACH

I COULD NOT HELP listening to Bob's prayer as he systematically thanked God for the number of people who would become Christians in different parts of the world. "Father, I thank You that in Africa about twenty thousand people will become Christians today." A little later he said, "Father, I thank You that in China about thirty thousand people will become Christians today." Then he asked God to protect these new Christians from persecution and to enable them to withstand whatever persecution came their way. "I thank You for the continual revival in South Korea and for the doors You are opening in the north."

Though I found myself agreeing with Bob's prayer, my mind once again turned to the idea that the Christian church worldwide is seeing the greatest growth ever.[1]

Bob's job as a missionary field director for the Pacific Rim countries is to manage and develop strategies and missions programs for these countries. Among the numerous leaders Bob has worked with is David Yonggi Cho of Seoul, Korea. Curious about Bob's prayer and the statistics he was reciting, I gave him a call later that day. I asked him, "Bob, in the countries you prayed about today, how many of the new converts will become Pentecostal?" Again, his number surprised me when he said, "About 60 percent."[2]

"I'm not sure that we can comprehend the numbers of

people who are coming to Christ and all of the reasons why. Christianity is the fastest-growing religious movement in the world, with a 6.9 percent growth rate per year. That compares to 2.7 percent for Islam, 2.2 percent for Hinduism, and 1.7 percent for Buddhism.[3]

Numerous denominations and Para church groups are pulling out the stops in their efforts to increase world evangelism. It seems that, with the turn of the millennium, countless organizations have a new vision, and many are setting wonderful goals. Dick Eastman of Every Home for Christ, David Bryant of Concerts of Prayer International, and many others are committed to enlisting and mobilizing the largest prayer movement in the history of the church. They, and we, are convinced that every revival has begun with prayer. Furthermore, the most creative means and effective technological equipment the church has ever used is now available. More than 2,500 Christian radio and television stations daily broadcast the gospel of Jesus Christ to a potential 4.6 billion of the world's population. Billy Graham conducted a crusade through satellites that may have been heard by as many as 2.5 billion people.[4] In the next few years, we will see a tremendous increase of propagating the gospel of Jesus Christ by satellite communication and the Internet.

Speaking of evangelism in our day, Neil Anderson writes:

> Not since the Day of Pentecost have we seen such a phenomenal growth of the church worldwide. For example, Africa was less than five percent Christian at the turn of the century; Africa is expected to be 50 percent Christian by the end of this millennium. In 1950 China had only one million believers; now it is estimated that one hundred million are coming to Christ annually. Indonesia is the world's most populated Muslim nation, but the percentage of Christians has been progressing so rapidly that the government won't release accurate figures. In 1900 South Korea did not have a single evangelical

church; in 1992 South Korea had 37,500 churches. Globally, the Holy Spirit has woven together a massive cooperative effort that could produce a harvest of at least one billion souls in the next five years. The church could be experiencing the first fruits of the greatest awakening it has ever known.[5]

No matter what we do or how we do it, we can know for certain that God is at work preparing a worldwide harvest. Jesus said, "No one can come to me unless the Father who sent me draws him" (John 6:44). God is drawing people to Christ from every village, tribe, community, city, and nation. A vast percentage of these people are also receiving the baptism in the Holy Spirit. Truly, we are living in one of the most exciting times in history.

PENTECOSTALISM CATCHES FIRE

Life magazine's special issue on the millennium ranked "the top 100 incredible discoveries, cataclysmic events, magnificent moments, of the past one thousand years." Number sixty-eight was "1906, Pentecostalism Catches Fire":

The Flame of Pentecostalism was first lighted when Charles Fox Parham declared in 1901 that speaking in tongues was a sign of baptism in the Holy Spirit. It might have sputtered if not for William Joseph Seymour, a black preacher who listened to Parham through an open door in his Houston Bible school. Soon, Seymour set out for Los Angeles, where his own baptism in the Spirit in 1906 brought him an enthusiastic following. Within two years of founding a mission in an abandoned church on Azusa Street, his multicultural ministry sent missionaries to twenty-five countries.

Pentecostalism is a religion of the heart. Since a personal experience with God is as important as doctrine, it is an adaptable faith; by the end of the 1960s, Protestants and Catholics have both begun to embrace the gifts of the Spirit in charismatic renewal movements....Today about a half billion people call themselves Pentecostal or charismatic, and Pentecostals alone outnumber Anglicans, Baptists, Lutherans, and Presbyterians combined. The Yoido Full Gospel Church in Seoul, South Korea, is now, at 700,000 strong, the largest Christian congregation on earth.[6]

The wave of the baptism in the Holy Spirit is literally touching every continent and every nation of the world. As we mentioned earlier, Brazil is seeing unprecedented Pentecostal growth. In his book *Fire From Heaven* Harvard University professor Harvey Cox writes:

> In 1992 a religious census carried on by a research center affiliated with the World Council of Churches revealed that in the previous three years approximately seven hundred new Pentecostal churches had opened in Rio....Despite population increases, only one saw Roman Catholic parish had been founded. The Pentecostal growth is most evident among the poorer communities. In the thirteen municipalities of Rio, there are three times as many Pentecostals in the peripheral favelas than in the more well-to-do and sophisticated southern zone, and Pentecostals are also three times more numerous among people with less than eight years of school and among those with the lowest wages. Once merely quick, the Pentecostal growth has now reached the proportions of a tidal wave. Besides, there are not many "nominal" or "nonobservant" Pentecostals. Scholars now estimate that on any given Sunday morning there are probably more Pentecostals at church in Brazil that there are Catholics at mass.[7]

This point is especially interesting, as many religious observers have historically considered Brazil a largely Catholic country.

Cox continues:

> A similar picture is emerging all over Latin America.
> In his book *Is Latin America Turning Protestant?* David
> Stoll pulls together statistics from a number of sources to
> show that non-Catholic Christianity is growing in many
> of the continent's countries at five or six times the rate of
> the general population. If the statistics in Brazil are any
> indication, 90 percent of this non-Catholic increase is
> Pentecostal. Stoll predicts that if current rates of growth
> continue, five or six Latin American countries will have
> non-Catholic—mostly Pentecostal—majorities by 2010.
> In several other nations the non-Catholic percentage of
> the population will have reached 30 to 40 percent.[8]

In a *Wall Street Journal* article, Pedro C. Moreno recently
wrote:

> The growth of Latin America's Evangelical population
> is staggering. In 1980, according to "Operation World,"
> by Patrick Johnstone, there were an estimated 21 mil-
> lion Evangelicals in the region, growing to 46 million by
> 1990. Today there are close to 60 million. Recent statis-
> tics show that Pentecostal—a subset of the Evangelical
> movement—account for two of every three Evangelicals
> in Latin America, and according to one estimate, nearly
> 40percent of the world's Pentecostals live in Latin Amer-
> ica.[9]

Moreno, who is a Bolivian lawyer, notes that the Pentecostal growth in Latin America crosses socioeconomic lines and
racial barriers.

Though most members of Pentecostal churches are poor
and uneducated, an increase of middle and upper-middle-
class members has brought the social classes together in a way
unfamiliar to Latin American people. White and black, mes-
tizo and Indian, educated and illiterate may be found holding

hands and even kissing during church services (something quite new for most Latin societies).

Pentecostals are generally credited with providing a sense of community to the masses migrating from the countryside to the cities. The British sociologist David Martin, in his book *Tongues of Fire: The Explosion of Protestantism in Latin America*, argues that the Pentecostal movement has created "free spaces" where a new ethos can develop. Many people have developed abilities within the church (leadership, organization, public speaking, etc.) that have helped them rise economically.[10]

WHY SUCH CHURCH GROWTH

Perhaps you have wondered why there is such unprecedented growth in Christianity and in Pentecostal/charismatic groups in particular. There are many possible answers.

First, God is pouring out His Spirit on all people. (See Acts 2:17.) Never has there been such great Christian growth, spiritual hunger, and worldwide interest in the message of Christ. We must continue to pray that doors will open in many nations around the world. Some of these doors have been closed because of religious persecution, political upheaval, or a dictatorial government leader who has prevented Christian outreach. Out of the approximately twelve thousand people groups in the world, approximately 1,700 of them still have not received an adequate witness about Jesus Christ.

We must also understand that in many of these "closed" countries, there may be a very strong church behind the scenes. China is a case in point, where, even though tragic persecution has occurred and the doors have remained closed, great church growth has also occurred. I recently spoke with a Christian leader from one of the closed countries. He told of amazing revival going on in his country. He said that he prayed that the doors from the West would stay closed for a little while longer. He did not think the church in his country could handle the affluence and aberrational teachings that might come. He said that the persecution many were receiving and the lack of material goods were of great concern to him; however, greater than that, he was frightened that the people would become distracted from their intense, pure devotion to Christ if the doors to their country suddenly opened.

God is truly pouring out his Spirit throughout the world in unprecedented ways. Joel prophesied that in the last days "Everyone who calls on the name of the Lord will be saved" (Acts 2:21).

Second, the twentieth century saw technological advancement, like no century before. To name just a few—automotive travel, air travel and space exploration, advanced weaponry, plastic, radio, television, computers, the Internet, e-mail, cellular telephones, penicillin, organ transplants, cloning. Think about it for a moment. Technology has grown beyond anyone's dreams. It would not be far afield to view Daniel's prophetic insights about the End Times—"Many will go here and there to increase knowledge" (Dan. 12:4)—as the twentieth century.

Christian denominations and church groups have been able to utilize much of what technology has provided. The world is much more reachable and the mandate to tell every tribe and nation about Jesus Christ is now possible. We could not say that a hundred years ago. In fact, we probably could not say that twenty years ago. This world has become a global village. We use wireless communications, all forms of transportation, and computers. We can publish books in a few days to give to tens of thousands. Most certainly, the church has been able to get to people faster, easier, and more efficiently than at any other time in history.

A third reason for such great church and Pentecostal growth is the increase of the evil in the world. The increase of evil has literally shocked many people into wanting reality, purity, and spiritual truth. Many look at the world they live in and become hopeless. They do not know how to get out of their rut of welfare and poverty, or they realize that no matter what they try, nothing brings real satisfaction or contentment.

One needs only to watch the evening news or look at the local newspaper to see the tremendous increase in violence, immoral behavior, divorce statistics, drugs, alcohol, and just plain confusion about life. In America we are allowing a million and a half abortions every year. This country will have to answer to God for that evil—and many others. This narcissistic society, in which people admire themselves, has also commonly accepted nihilism, in which many believe that traditional values are baseless. For some life has become meaningless.

Gary Bauer of the Family Research Council recently wrote:

> Every day, there is a new story on the predictable implications of our values meltdown. Today, the story comes out of little Mayville, New York, where an AIDS-infected thug intentionally had sex with as many young girls as possible in order to spread the HIV infection. Some of the girls were as young as 13 and the list of victims may eventually top one hundred.
>
> The predator in question is a drifter with no visible means of support, yet he was apparently able to seduce dozens of young women. Such a catastrophe would have been impossible in the America of even thirty years ago, yet today, even a little "conservative" town in upstate New York is not safe from the impact of the sexual revolution.[11]

We all could tell of some horrible event that has occurred in our communities, in our schools, or possibly even in our families. We live in a day where the downward spiral of evil will continue, people will become disillusioned, and family relationships will be destroyed. Out of their confusion, pain, and crises, many are crying out to God for help.

Jesus told us the conditions of the End Times, and we are

seeing those conditions fulfilled today. False Christs and false prophets will deceive many. (See Matthew 24:24.) There will be an increase in wickedness, and the love of most will grow cold (v. 12), and there will be wars and rumors of wars, famines, and earthquakes (vv. 6–7). People will be God-haters, and evil will increase. Life will become cheap—as we have seen through the practice of euthanasia and abortion. Paul's instructions to Timothy looks like the front page of our newspapers, "There will be terrible times in the last days. People will be lovers of themselves, lovers of money, boastful, proud, abusive, disobedient to their parents, ungrateful, unholy, without love, unforgiving, slanderous, without self-control, brutal, not lovers of the good, treacherous, rash, conceited, lovers of pleasure rather than lovers of God—having a form of godliness but denying its power" (2 Tim. 3:1–5).

To counteract the evil in the world and to make the gospel message powerful are the reasons God gave us the baptism in the Holy Spirit. This powerful *dunamis* will enable the church of Jesus Christ around the world to boldly impact every society. The evil influence of the world will not paralyze Spirit-filled Christians. They will have courage to stand against evil and fight through it. This baptism has no denominational tags or boundaries. It belongs to the church of Jesus Christ worldwide. If you are a child of God, you can have all that God offers.

Fourth, there has also been tremendous persecution is our generation. The stories of Christian persecution coming from China, Asia, parts of Eastern Europe, Iran, Iraq, Pakistan, Cuba, and many other nations are nothing less than horrific. H. B. London of Focus on the Family wrote in the *Pastor to Pastor* fact sheet:

- More than an estimated 160,000 believers were martyred in 1996, and countless others were subjected to unimaginable horrors (David C. Barrett, "Annual

Statistical Table on Global Mission," *International Bulletin of Missionary Research*, January 1997, p. 25).

- There are close to one hundred million martyrs in this "modern" twentieth century (*World Mission Digest*).

- There have been more people martyred for their faith in Jesus Christ in the twentieth century than in all the previous nineteen combined (James and Marti Hefley, *By Their Blood*).

- More people have died in circumstances related to their faith in this century than in all the twentieth century wars combined (statistical research of the WEF religious Liberty Commission).[12]

Terrible stories like the following are coming from many countries where Christian persecution is occurring. Mona Charen wrote in *The Washington Times* that:

Lai Man Peng was a twenty-two-year-old Chinese Christian evangelist. In 1994, at a meeting of one of China's "house churches" (a non-government-sanctioned prayer meeting), he and four other evangelists were seized by agents of the Public Security Bureau, China's KGB. In front of the congregation, Mr. Lai and the others were beaten severely. The security officers next handed the truncheons to the congregants and ordered them to beat the preachers, on pain of being beaten themselves. Mr. Lai was so badly injured that the security team feared he would die in their presence (leaving too much to explain), so they released him. He crawled and hobbled for several miles attempting to reach his home, but finally collapsed and died on the road. Such persecution is commonplace in China, where only a fraction of the estimated thirty million to seventy million Christians belong to government-approved sects. Amnesty International report cases of Christian women hung by their thumbs from wires and beaten with heavy rods, denied food and water and shocked with electric probes.[13]

The United Nations reports that the militant Islamic government of Central African Sudan has declared a systematic battle against Christians. Since 1982, three hundred thousand Sudanese Christians have been killed. Each year hundreds of Christian believers are sold into slavery and taken where they have to work as slaves or as concubines for their Muslim masters.[14]

Mona Charen reported in *The Washington Times* that "Pakistan recently passed a blasphemy law that forbids speaking or acting against the prophet Mohammed. The punishment for violators is death. A twelve-year-old Christian child was recently sentenced to death under this law and was freed from Pakistan only by international pressure. He is now hiding in a Western country with a bounty on his head similar to that which keeps Salman Rushdie on the run."[15]

Michael Horowitz, a Jew, tells why he is working so hard to help persecuted Christians:

> There is a man who lives with us who is the embodiment of Christian faith, and I'm in awe of it. He is from the Ethiopian Evangelical Church where he is the senior pastor. He is trying to get asylum into the United States and is meeting every possible roadblock you can imagine. Here is a man who has been jailed over twenty-five times for his faith. He's been tortured. On one occasion he was hanged upside down with hot oil poured on his feet. This is a man of abiding faith who will be tortured again and murdered if he is sent back to Ethiopia. But do you know what happened when we petitioned for asylum? The State Department sent a letter to the Immigration Service and said, "There's no persecution of Christians in Ethiopia."[16]

Interestingly, in spite of awful persecution, the church has grown in many of these countries. Even though in many cases Christians have had to go underground, they have become stronger and more committed. Persecution has intensified their faith. They are people of prayer, gifted at evangelism, and dedicated to the inerrant Word of God—and they believe in miracles. When new converts give their lives to Christ, many times they are prepared to die for their faith.[17]

I am pessimistic yet hopeful about the future. I am confident that the church of Jesus Christ will continue to grow. There will be a greater outpouring of the Holy Spirit than ever before, and the baptism in the Holy Spirit will become more and more the norm in the Christian church at large, not just in the Pentecostal/charismatic church. However, I am disheartened that this world will become more and more evil and disillusioned. Wars will increase, the economy will be divided, and sophisticated sinful inventions will be developed. Daniel said this about these days:

> Many will be purified, made spotless and refined, but the wicked will continue to be wicked. None of the wicked will understand, but those who are wise will understand.
>
> —DANIEL 12:10

LIFE THAT IS GREATER

The baptism in the Holy Spirit is a wonderful gift of God that will give us the power to reach a very deceived, confused, and disillusioned world. Not only do we need to demonstrate God's power but, through our daily lives, we also need to show the lost of the world that there is a wonderful God who loves them and deserves our praise and worship. People without Christ need to see a love they have never seen, a compassion they have never felt, a commitment and service they have never experienced, and a faith that is contagious.

This wonderful blessing from the Father will enable us to show and tell others that Jesus Christ is living in us. Our friends and neighbors need to see that our faith in Christ is the most precious and important aspect of our lives. Our faith is unique; there is not another faith in the world that has its kind of fulfillment, power, and sense of contentment. Our God is the only God who powerfully works in His children's lives. We can show those around us unique characteristics that nothing—or no one—else can show them.

A UNIQUE WORSHIP

Not long ago I was with the leaders of one of America's largest non-Pentecostal denominations. They said that the Pentecostal church is having a positive impact on them. Their people wanted the kind of music and worship that is coming out of many Pentecostal/charismatic groups and is sweeping the church world.

New choruses, beautiful hymns, and songs of worship are consistently being added to the church world. The reason for this is that the Holy Spirit encourages us to worship God and lift up the name of Jesus. Anglican archbishop William Temple said, "To worship is to quicken the conscience by the holiness of God, to feed the min with the truth of God, to purge the imagination by the beauty of God, to open the heart to the love of God, to devote the will to the purpose of God."[18]

Jack Hayford believes the church worldwide is in the second Reformation. It is his belief that Martin Luther's Protestant Reformation for the Roman Catholic Church was a reformation of doctrine only, not worship. Now Protestants are experiencing a reformation of worship.

God always responds when people reach out with hungry hearts and words to express their love to him in worship. This can happen privately when you are alone in your home or car, and it can happen corporately in a church service where the people in the congregation are unified in praise to God. The congregation senses God's presence filling the room.

A. W. Tozer said that "God wants worshippers before workers; indeed the only acceptable workers are those who have learned the lost art of worship.... The very stones would praise him if the need arose and a thousand legions of angels would leap to do his will."[19]

A UNIQUE LOVE

It should be no surprise to the Christian that the "love chapter" of 1 Corinthians is placed between chapter 12 and chapter 14, chapter 12 being about the gifts of the Spirit and chapter 14 being the explanation of how the gifts are to be used. Paul was inspired by the Holy Spirit to write about love in chapter 13. He said, "If I speak in the tongues of men and of angels, but have not love, I am only a resounding gong or a clanging cymbal" (1 Cor. 13:1).

The world needs to see Christians who are driven by love, governed by love, and motivated by love. Otherwise, what we try to do is in vain. We can have every charismatic gift there is, but if we do not demonstrate love, we will not see anyone change. It is confusing to people when they see someone apparently using spiritual gifts but the person is arrogant, full of pride, or uncaring in the way he or she treats people. We are to be motivated to do what we do because of our love for God. The love of Christ constrains us, the Spirit of God empowers us, and the very definition of God is that He is love. (See 1 John 4:16.)

The thing that makes missions organizations, service organizations like the Salvation Army, and drug rehabilitation programs like Teen Challenge so effective is that they demonstrate the love of Christ. They roll up their sleeves and get involved in people's pain and involve themselves in cultures that much of the world has ignored. They see through the eyes of Jesus, looking beyond a person's hang-ups and seeing the person whole. People are attracted to love that is demonstrated rather than just spoken. Everyone needs and hungers for God's pure love; and His love will change a person quicker than anything we can do.

John tells us "God is love. Whoever lives in love lives in God, and God in him. In this way, love is made complete among us so that we will have confidence on the day of judgment, because in this world we are like him" (1 John 4:16–17). To be an effective witness to those who need Christ, we must love in God's way. We must demonstrate God's character and treat others as God would treat them. How do we act when no one is looking? How do we treat people when we think no one is listening? Someone has said, "People do not care about how much you know until they know how much you care." If we treat people like God encourages us to, we will see our families, friends, and acquaintances come to Christ. They will want what we have.

How can you be a Christian who loves?

1. God is the start.

Knowing Him is the beginning. John tells us, "Dear friends, let us love one another, for love comes from God. Everyone who loves has been born of God and knows God. Whoever does not love does not know God, because God is love" (1 John 4:7–8). When we stop to think that God loves us in spite of our failures, sins, attitudes, and shortcomings, we must understand that He can love anyone. We, in turn, are to love people because we have God's Spirit dwelling in us. When we are full of the Spirit of God, a love beyond human compassion will be seen in our lives.

2. Make God's love your goal.

If you have difficulty loving a person or a group of people, make love your goal, because God's goals are good. Paul said, "I do not consider myself yet to have taken hold of it" (Phil.

3:13). That is, Paul had not reached his target yet, but he did have a goal. We can say to ourselves, "With God's help I will be a love channel." Paul prayed that his readers' love would abound "more and more in knowledge and depth of insight" (Phil. 1:9).

Our loving actions will often change people's lives. Recently Dr. James Dobson wrote about a high school teacher who had an interesting experience. The teacher had two students named Johnny. One was a happy child, and excellent student, a fine citizen. The other Johnny spent much of his time goofing off and making a nuisance of himself.

When the PTA held its first meeting of the year, a mother came up to this teacher and asked, "How's my son, Johnny, getting along?"

He assumed she was the mother of the better student and replied, "I can't tell you how much I enjoy him. I'm so glad he's in my class."

The next day the problem child came to the teacher and said, "My mom told me what you said about me last night. I haven't ever had a teacher who wanted me in his class."

That day he finished his assignments, and he even brought in his completed homework the next morning. A few weeks later the "problem" Johnny had become one of this teacher's hardest-working students—and one of his best friends. This misbehaving child's life was turned around all because he was mistakenly identified as a good student.[20]

If you have difficulty loving someone because that person has mistreated you or spoken harshly about you or to you, you can say in your heart that it is your goal to love that person in Jesus' name. This does not mean that you should stay involved in physically harmful relationships, but you can show the person the love of God. The Holy Spirit will give you the strength to do so.

3. Love by faith.

We do not always feel like doing or saying the loving thing or acting in loving ways. But we can love by faith. We can do acts of love, works of love, and speak in loving ways regardless of our feelings. Our emotions are not always in agreement with our decisions. I do not *feel* like working every day, but I do. I might not even *feel* like praying or reading my Bible every day, but I do. Regardless of how I feel, I decide to do the right thing. Showing all people the love of God is the right thing.

James Dobson wrote that he heard of a wedding ceremony during which the bride and groom pledged to stay married as long as they continued to love each other. Dobson said this about that couple:

> I hope they both know good divorce attorneys, because they're going to need them. Relationships based on feelings are ephemeral and transitory. The only real stability in marriage is produced by firm commitments that hold two people steady when emotions are fluctuating wildly. Without this determination to cement human relationships, they are destined to disintegrate.
>
> Emotion might be thought of as the caboose on a train. A committed will is the engine that pulls the relationship through all the ups and downs of everyday living.[21]

A UNIQUE COMPASSION

Along with the tremendous outpouring of the Holy Spirit, we are seeing a great increase and demonstration of compassion. When you look at times of revival in church history, you will see wonderful acts of compassion. The church becomes conscious of the needs of society—the poor, the hurting, the less fortunate, those who are suffering. This is a result of Christ's love being poured into the church through renewal and through the Spirit. Compassion—faith translated into action—is a spiritual barometer of a person's spiritual fullness.

You can grow in your compassion for people. Scripture tells us that "Jesus went through all the towns and villages, teaching in their synagogues, preaching the good news of the kingdom and healing every disease and sickness. When he saw the crowds, he had compassion on them, because they were harassed and helpless, like sheep without a shepherd" (Matt. 9:35–36). If we see people's need, we will feel compassion to do something about it.

Jesus saw those in need.

When we get involved in people's lives or visit a part of the city that has great privation, we will see the pain, heartache, and human suffering that are a part of so many people's lives today. But we have to want to see. Each of us can live in his or her own private world ignoring others' pain. It takes effort to see and hear what is going on in someone else's life.

Jesus felt compassion.

When we endeavor to see and hear what is really going on in a person's life, we will have an emotional response—often we will feel compassion. When I was in graduate school for a counseling degree, I was required to complete an internship. I decided to serve my internship as a probation officer with young people under the age of sixteen. Though I experienced a good deal of success with most of my cases, I had one twelve or thirteen-year-old boy who just could not seem to do anything right.

One day I decided to visit the boy's home. After finding his road on a map, I drove down the dirt road looking for the house. I did not find a house but noticed a small building covered with black tar paper in the middle of a field. Out of the roof of the building was a smoking silver chimney. I thought, *This cannot be where Tim lives.* But I turned down the muddy driveway, parked, and walked down a short path to the door. I knocked a few times, and Tim answered the door.

"Hello, Tim. I just wanted to see how you're doing," I quickly blurted out. As I looked at this young, hardened boy, I could not help noticing the room behind him. A woodstove doubled as a cooking stove. Old food and dirty dishes were stacked on top of it. Newspapers were piled up around the walls. I caught a glimpse of his bedroom, where an old mattress lay on the floor with a dirty blanket wadded up on top of it. The room smelled bad, and it was difficult for me to comprehend that someone lived in such a place.

Tim looked at me and said, "Yeah, what do you want?"

I said, "I wanted to visit where you lived and meet your family."

From a side room his mother walked out. She looked tired and just as hard as her son. After visiting with Tim and his mother for a few minutes, I drove back to the clean office building where the probation department was located. I told one of the officers about visiting Tim and his mother. The officer then informed me that Tim's mother was the town prostitute.

When I found this out and thought about Tim's living conditions, my disappointment toward him changed. I now understood why Tim was so hard and disobedient. He simply did not care anymore. Life had been terribly rough on this young boy, and I was compelled to find a way to show him that life could be different and that there were people who sincerely cared about him and his future.

My feelings changed because I saw Tim in his tragic condition. I now felt a new compassion. This motivated me to be more attentive to Tim's unique needs and to be careful to understand his resistance to change. As a result, he improved and accepted favorably his probation.

When we take the time to see, we feel. The world is full of people who need to sense our compassion, not our judgment and condemnation. The Spirit of God who lives in every believer wants us to see people the way He sees people. They are "harassed and helpless, like sheep without a shepherd."

Jesus acted. "Jesus went...teaching...preaching the good

news of the kingdom and healing every disease and sickness" (Matt. 9:35). When we see we will feel and, with God's help, do something about it. "What good is it, my brothers, if a man claims to have faith but has no deeds?.... In the same way, faith by itself, if it is not accompanied by action, is dead" (James 2:14, 17).

People need to see our Christian compassion in what we do. We can do something about pain and suffering. We can go to people who have been rejected by the world and marked as hopeless. We can dig deeper, work harder, and last longer in the occupation of helping people because we are motivated and energized by the Holy Spirit.

A UNIQUE SACRIFICE

Sacrifice is an attribute that was evident in the early church. It is evident in the church today as well. Scripture tells us that in the early church, "All the believers were one in heart and mind. No one claimed that any of his possessions was his own, but they shared everything they had" (Acts 4:32). Sacrifice is a common feature of those in God's kingdom. It is common to hear of Christians who are leaving homes, material possessions, and occupations to give of themselves sacrificially. It does not make sense to those in the world who believe in looking out for *number one*. Who would leave parents, homes, and successful careers to go to a foreign culture and live in uncomfortable conditions? People do not commonly do that just because they are good people. They do it because they have been moved upon by the Holy Spirit and sacrifice has become part of their lives. When others around them see their sacrifice, they wonder, *Why do they do that? What makes them so committed?*

Malcolm Muggeridge said, "Christians are often accused of being morbid when they talk of the joy of sacrificing. I think it is one of the deepest truths of the Christian religion. Far from being a source of sadness, sacrifice is a great joy and source of illumination—perhaps the greatest of all. I also think that to live modestly is always a richer experience because you are living like the majority of people."[22] The great missionary David Livingstone had the right perspective when he said, "I never made a sacrifice. We ought not to talk of sacrifice when we remember the great sacrifice that he made who left his Father's throne on high to give himself for us."[23]

A Unique Service

The Spirit-filled person lives a life of service. Jesus did not come to be served, but to serve. (See Mark 10:45.) He is our example, and the Holy Spirit helps us serve with joy. In our own nature we want to lead, take charge, run the program, or be the boss. God desperately needs leaders in his church, but leadership style is to be the greatest servant of all. We have to be content with being last, sitting in the back of the room, or being the first to react when there is a need. Being a servant in a world of competition is tough, but it is the way God's kingdom operates—and it will for eternity.

When those around you see the fruit of the Spirit in your life, sense the love and compassion of God in your heart, and believe that you are a servant of Jesus Christ, they will be attracted to the God you serve. The baptism in the Holy Spirit will enable you to serve others—your family, your employer, your neighbor, and your church. It will empower you to have a unique compassion and, as a result, be a greater witness.

Jesus was concerned that the early disciples wait for the filling of the Holy Spirit before beginning a lifelong ministry. He wanted them to have every available advantage to do all that they could do for God's kingdom. I am reminded of a credit card commercial that says, "Don't leave home without it." Similarly, ministry should not begin until we have all the power that God freely gives.

The other day I received an e-mail message from a young man who lives in a city about fifty miles from the city where I live. This was his request:

> My name is [name deleted]. This is going to sound strange, but I want to receive the baptism of the Holy Spirit. I've been praying for it for about five months now. I'm not from an Assemblies of God denomination. I'm from a [denomination's name deleted] background. I've been studying this whole awesome issue, and it's awesome. I'm 19 years old, and I go to school in [city deleted], Missouri. I attend school at [college name deleted]. I'm studying to become a preacher of the Word of God. I've been praying for sometime now, but I need hands laid on me and to be prayed for. I've attended a few different Assembly of God churches over the past few months just trying to understand what it is about. I've read a few books concerning the issue, and I know now that it is true and biblically accurate. I desire it, and I have read different testimonies of how some people have received this. The Bible and other testimonies show that the laying on of hands is another way to receive it. I just would like someone to give me a call. Honestly, I will drive to your city and meet with anyone willing to lay hands on me for this awesome gift from God. I would do it tomorrow afternoon after classes if I received a call back tonight or even tomorrow morning. I just desire for someone to call me and talk to me. My number is [number deleted]. Thank you for your time, and God bless anyone who may read this.

When I read this young man's letter and sensed the hunger in his heart, I immediately telephoned him. He was not in his room, so I called back the next day and left a message that I had tried to reach him. Within a few days one of my staff members did reach him, and we asked him to meet with some college students who wanted to pray for him. He came, and his prayers were answered. When the students prayed for him, he began praying in a language he had never learned. With all of his heart, he worshiped God in tongues for over an hour. He was overjoyed, full of boldness, and only God knows where his future will take him.

Numerous people along the way dropped what they were doing to try to serve the young man. As a result, God used one servant after another to answer the desire of his young heart.

MIRACLE IN NAGALAND

For years Christians in Nagaland, East India, prayed that Billy Graham would visit them. They had heard about him from missionaries and hungered to see and hear him in their own country. Finally, in November 1972, he scheduled a crusade in an area called "hills of the Headhunters." Amid tremendous difficulties that nearly resulted in the crusade being canceled, the believers prayed and the crusade saw a tremendous number of people give their lives to Christ.

Many credited missionary Mark Buntain of Calcutta, India, for his role in preparing hearts for Graham's crusade. Six years earlier Mark had received an invitation to speak to a large crowed in Nagaland. Like Graham, he had also faced an obstacle. This was a restricted area, and foreigners needed a permit to travel there. Mark was not able to get one, so he had to send word back that, regrettably, it was impossible for him to attend the conference.

He lay awake at night trying to discern God's will. One morning at 4:00, Mark jumped out of bed and said to his wife, Huldah, "I'm going to Nagaland."

Huldah, said, "Mark, you can't go. You don't have a permit. They won't let you on the plane."

"God has told me to go, and I'm going," he responded.

He packed his bag and set out for the airport. The rest was a miracle—how he was issued a ticket and boarded the plan without anyone asking for a permit, how he was later issued a permit to travel many back roads to the town of Mukokchung, where the conference was being held.

The people prayed all night that Mark would come. At dawn they heard his jeep climbing up the mountain. They came out of their tents to see if God had answered their prayers.

When Mark stepped out of the jeep, he heard a roar of celebration. "Hallelujah!" the people shouted.

More than ten thousand people were in attendance. Some had walked two or three days over mountains to attend the conference.

That night Mark preached for one hour. Afterward, however, they said his message was too short.

A visiting minister talked to Mark before the next evening's service and said, "They don't know about the Holy Spirit." He encouraged Mark, "Please speak on the Holy Spirit."

Mark preached for three hours that night, and still the people wanted more. After his sermon, he began to pray and speak in tongues. Unbeknown to Mark, he was actually speaking in a known tongue—the crowd's native language. It was a language familiar to everyone—a mixture of dialects—and Mark was speaking to them about the baptism in the Holy Spirit. They knew they were witnessing a miracle. There was no way Mark could have known their language. That was the birth of many churches in the region—churches that later participated in Graham's crusade.[24]

We could tell you story after story about how the Holy Spirit continues to use people. The Holy Spirit is active throughout the world, and He wants to be completely active in your life.

Are you hungry for more of God? I pray that you will tell God that you are eager to have all that He has for you. Seek God about this blessing. If you do not receive it the first time, do not be discouraged. Remember that the early church had a time of waiting before they received the promised gift. If you have received the blessing, know that this experience brings the believer into a relationship with the Spirit that is to be renewed and maintained. We preserve this sensitivity by our prayer life, our Christian witness, and our worship, and by living a holy life. As you serve God, you will be a conduit of God's passion, love, caring, and power. As you pour yourself out in service to others, the Lord will refill you.

"The Blessing" is given so that you will have the power to witness to a world that desperately needs to know our wonderful God of love.

NOTES

Preface

1. George Barna, *The Second Coming of the Church* (Dallas: Word, 1998): quoted in *Current Thoughts and Trends* 14, no. 3 (March 1998), 31.

2. Ron Sellers, "Nine Global Trends in Religion," *Futurist 32*, no. 1 (January/February 1998), 20-25; quoted in *Current Thoughts and Trends* 14, no. 3 (March 1998), 27.

3. Michael Green and R. Paul Stevens, *New Testament Spirituality* (London: Eagle, 1994), 4.

Chapter 1
The Outpouring: The Rediscovery of Azusa and Its Significance

1. Diane's depression had weakened her emotionally and physically. A common characteristic of people in clinical depression is for them to avoid interaction. It is too difficult to try to be pleasant and have conversations. Sometimes the depressed person feels overwhelming sadness or panic, wants to be left alone, or lacks the desire or energy to even get out of bed.

2. Parham's home in Topeka, Kansas, was called "Stone's Folly" because the builder, Erastus R. Stone, suffered financial reverses in the 1880s before the mansion was completed.

3. The Bible school was later called Bethel Bible School. The school only operated until July 1901.

4. Wayne Warner, *Pentecostal Evangel*, 30 December 1990, 7.

5. The Scripture references the group referred to were Acts 2:4; 10:46; 19:6; 1 Corinthians 14:1-33. For more on Parham see Vinson Synan, *The Holiness Pentecostal Movement in the United States* (Grand Rapids: Eerdmans, 1971), 51–53.

6. Synan, *The Holiness Pentecostal Movement in the United States*, 101.

7. Ibid.

8. "We Rank the Top 100 Incredible Discoveries, Cataclysmic Events, Magnificent Moments, of the Past 1,000 Years," *Life, The Millennium*, special issue (Fall 1997).

9. Synan, *The Holiness Pentecostal Movement in the United States*, 102. Pentecostal historian Wayne Warner recently commented to me that there was the possibility that one of the students did not receive the experience and in fact was critical of the others. On the revival, see also Gary B. McGee, "Azusa Street Revival," in *Dictionary of Pentecostal and Charismatic Movements*, ed. Stanley M. Burgess and Gary B. McGee (Grand Rapids: Zondervan, 1988), 32.

10. Ibid., 102.

11. Ibid.

12. Ibid.

13. Ibid.

14. Stanley M. Horton, *Heritage* (Fall 1982), 2.

15. Ibid.

16. Ibid.

17. I define Charismatics as people who have come from traditional denominations (e.g., Baptist, Methodist, Presbyterian, Roman Catholic) and have received the experience called the baptism in the Holy Spirit. Often they have chosen to remain in their denomination, limiting their expression of the gifts of the Holy Spirit to private times unless their churches have permitted them to use their gifts publicly. Pentecostals are those who have received the baptism in the Holy Spirit and are a part of a Pentecostal fellowship or denomination.

18. Russell P. Spittler, "Implicit Values in Pentecostal Missions," *Missiology: An International Review*, October 1988, 410. It should also be noted that by the end of the twentieth century most Christians will live in the Southern Hemisphere, most will belong to the two-thirds world, and most will reflect a Pentecostal spirituality (411).

19. David Barrett, "Status of Global Mission, 1997, in Context of 20th and 21st Centuries," *World Evangelization*, no. 78, Lausanne Committee for World Evangelization, Norway (May 1997), 17.

20. Harvey Cox, *Fire from Heaven* (Reading, MA: Addison-Wesley, 1995), 15.

21. Spittler, "Implicit Values in Pentecostal Missions," 421.

22. David Miller, "Latin America's Sweeping Revival," *Charisma*, June 1996, 32–38: quoted in *Current Thoughts and Trends* 12, no. 4 (August 1996), 28.

Chapter 2
The Blessing: The Baptism of the Holy Spirit

1. Charles G. Finney, *Memoirs* (New York: Revell, 1876), 20-21.

2. Ibid., 25.

3. J. Rodman Williams, *Renewal Theology*, vol. 2 (Grand Rapids: Zondervan, 1988), 203.

4. See also Mark 1:8; Luke 3:16; John 1:33; Acts 1:5; 11:16.

5. Billy Graham, *The Holy Spirit* (Dallas: Word, 1988), xiv-xv.

6. See *The Full Life Study Bible* (Grand Rapids: Zondervan, 1992), 1668-69.

7. Robert P. Menzies, "The Distinctive Character of Luke's Pneumatology," *Paraclete* (Fall 1991), 18.

8. Russell P. Spittler, "Implicit Values in Pentecostal Missions," *Missiology: An International Review*, October 1988, 420.

9. Adapted from "The Holy Spirit Pleads, Share the Gospel in the North, Too," *Mountain Movers*, October 1996, 11.

10. Gordon Chilvers, "Ye Shall be Witnesses," *Paraclete* (Winter 1971), 5.

11. Arthur T. Pierson, *The Acts of the Holy Spirit* (London: Morgan and Scott, n.d.), 121-22: quoted in Henry Barclay Swete, *The Holy Spirit in the New Testament* (London: Macmillan, 1909), 327.

12. Ibid. , 179.

13. Swete, *The Holy Spirit in the New Testament*, 319.

14. Charles W. Conn, *Pillars of Pentecost* (Cleveland, TN: Pathway Press, 1956), 28.

15. Quoted in Vinson Synan, *Aspects of Pentecostal-Charismatic Origins* (South Plainfield, NJ: Logos, 1975), 31.

16. Quoted in Gwen Jones, Ron Rowden, and Mel Surface, eds., *Higher Goals: National Church Growth Convention Digest* (Springfield, MO: Gospel Publishing House, 1978), v.

17. Ray H. Hughes, *Church of God Distinctives* (Cleveland, TN: Pathway Press, 1968), 63.

18. Grant L. McClung Jr., *Azusa Street and Beyond* (South Plainfield, NJ: Logos, 1986), 74.

Chapter 3
The Evidence: Speaking in Tongues

1. Adapted from Lloyd Christiansen, "When Unknown Tongues Are Not Unknown," *Pentecostal Evangel*, 30 December 1990, 7.

2. Adapted from Denny Miller, "A Brand-New Tongue," *Pentecostal Evangel*, 30 March 1997, 18.

3. I am not certain about the location of the 120. Most think it was the Upper Room, which seemed to be their headquarters (Acts 1:13). Some, however, because of Peter's statement that it was "only nine in the morning"—Acts 2:15, think that they were in the temple. The disciples habitually were in the temple at the hours of prayer.

4. John Sherrill, *They Speak with Other Tongues* (1964; reprint, Grand Rapids: Revell, 1993), 107-8.

5. Ibid., 109.

6. Stanley M. Horton, *The Book of Acts: The Wind of the Spirit* (Springfield, MO: Gospel Publishing House, 1996), 33.

7. Ibid., 105.

8. Ibid., 106.

9. Quoted in Stanley M. Horton, *Systematic Theology* (Springfield, MO: Logion Press, 1994), 441.

10. Ibid., 223.

11. J. H. E. Hull, *The Holy Spirit in the Acts of the Apostles* (London: Lutterworth, 1967), 110.

12. Including *Codex Bezae (D)* (a papyrus from the third or fourth century A.D.), plus Syriac and Sahidic versions originating in the second and third

centuries A.D.

13. Horton, *The Book of Acts*, 119–20.

14. Gordon D. Fee, *The First Epistle to the Corinthians, New International Commentary on the New Testament* (Grand Rapids: Eerdmans, 1987), 656–57.

15. *Spirit Filled Life Bible*, Jack W. Hayford, gen. ed. (Nashville: Thomas Nelson, 1991), 1740.

16. Over the years of Graham's crusade ministry, all charismatic, Pentecostal and evangelical denominations have enjoyed rich friendship with Dr. Graham.

17. Sherrill, *They Speak With Other Tongues*, 84.

18. Michael P. Hamilton, *The Charismatic Movement* (Grand Rapids: Eerdmans, 1975), 23.

Chapter 4
The Overflow: Being Filled With the Holy Spirit

1. Story abridged from Charles E. Greenaway, "I Have Planted Three Seeds," *Pentecostal Evangel*, 1 March 1970, 8–9.

2. Edyth Draper, *Draper's Book of Quotations for the Christian World* (Wheaton, IL: Tyndale, 1992), 395.

3. George Sweeting, *Great Quotes and Illustrations* (Dallas Word, 1985), 174.

4. Ibid., 173.

5. Story adapted from David Wilkerson, *The Cross and the Switchblade* (Westwood, NJ: Spire Books, 1964), 7.

6. Ibid., 61–62.

7. James Gilchrist Lawson, *Deeper Experiences of Famous Christians* (Anderson, IN: Warner Press, 1911; reprint 1981), 246–47.

8. Sweeting, *Great Quotes*, 171.

9. Dwight L. Moody, *Notes from My Bible* (Chicago: Revell, 1895), 166.

10. Anthony J. Ruspantini, *Quoting Spurgeon* (Grand Rapids: Baker, 1994), 63.

11. Glen Van Ekeren, *Speaker's Sourcebook II* (Englewood Cliffs, NJ: Prentice Hall, 1994), 246.

12. George Barna, "A Fountain of Sand," *The Barna Report* 1, no. 3, 2.

13. George Barna, "The Top 100: Part 2," *The Barna Report*, July/August 1997, 2.

14. Quoted in Ted W. Engstrom and Norman B. Rohrer, *Making the Right Choices* (Nashville: Thomas Nelson, 1993), 9.

15. Ibid.

16. Ibid., xi.

17. David Lim, *Spiritual Gifts: A Fresh Look* (Springfield, MO: Gospel Publishing House, 1991), 224.

18. William Barclay, *The Letters to the Galatians and Ephesians, The Daily*

Study Bible (Philadelphia: Westminster Press, 1976), 49–50.

19. Stephen Neill, *The Christian Character* (New York: Association Press, 1955), 22: quoted in Billy Graham, *The Holy Spirit* (Dallas: Word, 1988), 249.

20. Ibid., 21.

21. Charles Allen, *The Miracle of the Holy Spirit* (Old Tappan, NJ: Revell, 1974), 56.

22. Barclay, *Galatians and Ephesians*, 50.

23. Quoted in Graham, *Holy Spirit*, 256.

24. See Barclay, *Galatians and Ephesians*, 51.

25. Ibid.

26. Allen, *Miracle of the Holy Spirit*, 60.

27. Ibid.

28. Ibid.

29. Graham, *Holy Spirit*, 266.

30. *The Full Life Study Bible* (Grand Rapids: Zondervan, 1992), 1841.

31. Ibid.

32. Barclay, *Galatians and Ephesians*, 52.

33. Raymond V. Edman, *They Found the Secret* (Grand Rapids: Zondervan, 1960), 98.

34. Quoted in Graham, *Holy Spirit*, 277.

35. Ibid.

36. See Barclay, *Galatians and Ephesians*, 52.

37. Manford George Gutzke, *The Fruit of the Spirit* (Atlanta: The Bible for You, n.d.), 10–11.

38. Sweeting, *Great Quotes*, 51.

39. Ibid., 140.

Chapter 5
The Signs: Signs and Wonders

1. Assemblies of God missionary Denny Miller.

2. David Lim, *Spiritual Gifts: A Fresh Look* (Springfield, MO: Gospel Publishing House, 1991), 70.

3. Ralph W. Harris, *Acts Today: Signs and Wonders of the Holy Spirit* (Springfield, MO: Gospel Publishing House, 1996), 10.

4. Many scholars question the authenticity of vv. 9–20, primarily because of omission of these verses in some of the earliest manuscripts and because their style is somewhat different from the rest of Mark. However, Christian writers of the second century, such as Justin Martyr, Irenaeus, and Tatian, testify to the inclusion of these verses, and the earliest translations, such as the Latin, Syriac, and Coptic, all include them. In any case, the passage does reflect the experience and expectation of the early church concerning the practice of charismatic gifts, and the question of its authenticity should remain open. (This explanation of Mark 16:9–20 is taken from the *Spirit*

Filled Life Bible, Jack W. Hayford, gen. ed. [Nashville: Thomas Nelson, 1991], 1502.) I believe that any reading that is authenticated by the majority of the ancient manuscripts is presumable to be the genuine writing of the biblical author.

5. *Spirit-Filled Life Bible*, 1502: "The signs accredit the gospel message, and cannot be limited to the apostolic age, any more than the Lord's commission to carry the gospel throughout the world. The signs, therefore, confirm the ministries of Christ's ambassadors in every generation. Casting out demons, speaking in tongues, and healing all appear in other passages in the NT, and there is no scriptural warrant for their cessation before the Lord returns. Taking up serpents does not refer to handling snakes in religious ceremonies, but casting them away without being harmed. (See Acts 28:3–6.) The Greek verb *airo*, 'take up,' can also mean 'remove,' 'take away,' or 'cast away." (See Matthew 14:12; Luke 11:52; 1 Corinthians 5:2; Ephesians 4:31.) Similarly, a servant of the Lord may look for divine protection in matters pertaining to food and drink. Many missionaries have testified to God's miraculous protection in heathen territories, where they experienced no ill effects from impure food and drink. All of the signs listed here have occurred repeatedly in Christian history."

6. Harvey Cox, *Fire from Heaven* (Reading, MA: Addison-Wesley, 1995) 222.

7. Adapted from David Yonggi Cho, *When Buddha Didn't Answer* (Springfield, MO: Assemblies of God Division of Foreign Missions), undated brochure.

8. Cessationists believe that the gifts of the Spirit ended with the first-century church. They claim that there is no longer any need for such gifts because we now have the Bible.

9. Jack Deere, *Surprised by the Spirit* (Grand Rapids: Zondervan, 1993), 55–56.

10. Larry Sibley, *Classic Quotes on Contemporary Issues* (Wheaton, IL: Harold Shaw, 1997), 42.

11. Robert Spence, "Scientist Gives Credit to God," *Pentecostal Evangel*, 26 June 1988, 10.

Chapter 6
The Charisma: Spiritual Gifts

1. To protect confidentiality, the name has been changed. Abridged from the *Pentecostal Evangel*.

2. Bruce Bugbee, *What You Do Best* (Grand Rapids: Zondervan, 1996), 59-60.

3. Fee writes, "The NIV breaks the paragraph into subparagraphs—as part of its (commendable) attempt to be 'international' (a readable translation for those for whom English is a second language). But in this case the two parts need to be seen together or too much is lost" (Gordon D. Fee, *The First Epistle*

to the Corinthians, NICNT [Grand Rapids: Eerdmans, 1987]. 584).

4. Ibid.

5. Ibid., 584–85.

6. Quoted in J. David Schmidt, *Changes that Count*, 42: a teaching manual on church growth published at 100 W. Roosevelt, Suite B6, Wheaton, IL 60187.

7. Frederic L. Godet, *Commentary on First Corinthians*, vol. 2 (Edinburgh: T. & T. Clark, 1886), 173.

8. Ronald Y. K. Fung, "Ministry, Community and Spiritual Gifts," *Evangelical Quarterly*, 20 January 1984, 15.

9. Please note that I recommend referring people to trained Christian professionals for counseling when they have psychological or severe emotional difficulties. Pastors and fellow church members can be a great asset by providing encouragement and prayer support to both the persons seeking help and to the professionals counseling them.

10. George Barna, "The Top 100: Part 1," *The Barna Report*, July-August 1997.

11. George Barna, "The Top 100: Part 2," *The Barna Report*, July-August 1997.

12. Schmidt, *Changes That Count*, 40.

13. Ibid.

14. Ibid., 41.

15. Ibid.

16. Adapted from Don and Terri Triplett, "Facing Down the Enemy," *Mountain Movers*, October 1997, 16–17.

17. Arnold Bittlinger, *Gifts and Graces: A Commentary on First Corinthians 12 to 14* (Grand Rapids: Eerdmans, 1967), 20.

18. David Lim, *Spiritual Gifts in the Work of the Ministry Today* (Springfield, MO: Gospel Publishing House, 1963), 62.

19. Ibid., 64.

20. Donald Gee, *Spiritual Gifts in the Work of the Ministry Today* (Springfield, MO: Gospel Publishing House, 1963), 29.

21. Donald Gee, *Concerning Spiritual Gifts* (Springfield, MO: Gospel Publishing House, (Springfield, MO: Gospel Publishing House, 1994), 54.

22. Harold Horton, *Gifts of the Spirit* (London: Assemblies of God Publishing House, 1962), 178.

23. It would be helpful to read my book *The Battle: Defeating the Enemies of Your Soul*, to understand Satan's abilities, his strategy, his hatred for the church, and how he has been defeated by what Jesus did on the cross.

24. Thomas L. Holdcroft, *The Holy Spirit: A Pentecostal Interpretation* (Springfield, MO: Gospel Publishing House, 1979), 150.

25. *Spirit-Filled Life Bible*, Jack W. Hayford, gen. ed. (Nashville: Thomas Nelson, 1991), 1737.

26. *The Full Life Study Bible* (Grand Rapids: Zondervan, 1992), 1,656.

27. Lim, *Spiritual Gifts*, 85.

Chapter 7
The Experience: What Must I Do?

1. At times when people are being baptized in the Holy Spirit, they need encouragement to worship God out loud. It is not uncommon for people to try to remain quiet because they think it is proper or they are shy, when emotionally they feel like speaking. Giving them permission to speak is often all the encouragement they need to speak in the language God has given them.

2. This experience happened at Cedar Park Assembly of God in Bothell, Washington. Dr. Joseph Fuiten is the pastor.

3. Reinhard Bonnke, *The Holy Spirit Baptism* (Sacramento: Reinhard Bonnke Ministries, n.d.), 23. Available through Reinhard Bonnke Ministries, Inc., P.O. Box 277440, Sacramento, CA 95827.

4. Ibid., 12.

5. Acts 1:5: "For John baptized with water, but in a few days you will be baptized with the Holy Spirit." The preposition *with* is the translation of the Greek word *en* and is often translated as "in." For this reason many prefer the rendering "...you will be baptized *in* the Holy Spirit." Luke uses several terms to describe this experience. He notes that people were "filled with the Holy Spirit"—Acts 2:4; 9:17, that "they received the Holy Spirit" (8:17), that "the Holy Spirit came on [them]" (10:44), that "the gift of the Holy Spirit came on them" (19:6). These are all then fundamental equivalents of Jesus' promise that the church would `be baptized with the Holy Spirit."

6. George Sweeting, *Great Quotes and Illustrations* (Dallas: Word, 1985), 139.

7. Edythe Draper, *Draper's Book of Quotations for the Christian World* (Wheaton, IL: Tyndale, 1992), 314.

8. Anthony J. Ruspantini, *Quoting Spurgeon* (Grand Rapids: Baker, 1994), 77.

9. Draper, *Draper's Book of Quotations*, 313.

10. Bonnke, *Holy Spirit Baptism*, 24.

11. Draper, *Draper's Book of Quotations*, 316.

12. John Sherrill, *They Speak With Other Tongues* (1964; reprint, Grand Rapids: Revell, 1993), 115.

13. Draper, *Draper's Book of Quotations*, 315.

14. Sweeting, *Great Quotes*, 215.

15. Ibid., 116–17.

16. Draper, *Draper's Book of Quotations*, 315.

17. Adapted from Wayne Warner, "When Dr. Willis Hoover Took a Stand in Chile," *Pentecostal Evangel*, 9 March 1997, 28.

Chapter 8
The Dangers: Excesses and Extremes

1. "Charlatans in the Church," *U.S. News & World Report*, 29 March 1993, 51.

2. Ibid.

3. Ibid.

4. Ibid.

5. Jack Deere, *Surprised by the Power of the Spirit* (Grand Rapids: Zondervan, 1993), 80.

6. Quoted in John Van Diest, *Unsolved Miracles* (Sisters, OR: Multnomah, 1997), 91.

7. Deere, *Surprised by the Power of the Spirit*, 78.

8. Jonathan Edwards, *The Distinguishing Marks of a Work of the Spirit of God* (Boston: S. Kneeland and T. Green, 1741): quoted in Richard and Kathryn Riss, *Images of Revival* (Shippensburg, PA: Revival Press, Destiny Image Publishers, 1997), 20.

9. John Wesley's journal, July 7, 1739, in Nehemiah Curnock, ed., *The Journal of the Rev. John Wesley, a.m.*, Vol. 2 (London: Charles H. Kelly, 1909–16), 239–40.

10. James Patterson Gledstone, *The Life and Travels of George Whitefield, M.A.* (London: Longmans, Green, and Co., 1871), 215.

11. John Wesley's journal, July 19, 1757 (Curnock ed.), 2:385.

12. John Wesley's journal, in Thomas Jackson, ed., *The Works of John Wesley*, vol. 2 (Grand Rapids: Zondervan, 1958–59), 499–500.

13. John Wesley's journal, August 6, 1759 (Curnock ed.), 4:344–47.

14. Charles G. Finney, *Memoirs* (New York: A. S. Barnes, 1976), 44–45.

15. Ibid., 103.

16. Jonathan Edwards, *The Distinguishing Marks of a Work of the Spirit of God*, in *The Great Awakening*, ed. C. C. Goen (New Haven: Yale University Press, 1972), 229.

17. Edward's points of evidence of revival and his comments were abridged from Robert Stallman's untitled article in *Contending for the Faith, Theological Journal of Central Bible College*, Springfield, MO, Summer 1995.

18. William Barclay, *The Letters to the Corinthians, The Daily Study Bible* (Philadelphia: Westminster Press, 1975), 114–15.

19. Sweeting, *Great Quotes*, 172.

20. Gordon D. Fee, *The First Epistle to the Corinthians*, NICNT (Grand Rapids: Eerdmans, 1987), 688.

21. Anthony J. Ruspantini, *Quoting Spurgeon* (Grand Rapids: Baker, 1994), 76.

22. Quoted in John Phillips, *Exploring the Future* (Neptune, NJ: Loizeaux Brothers, 1992), 232.

23. Ibid., 232–33.

24. *The Full Life Study Bible* (Grand Rapids: Zondervan, 1992), 1508.

25. Ibid., 1509.

Chapter 9
The Benefits: Boldness and Strength

1. The prayer meeting in which this story took place was comprised of a small group of men who gathered on Saturday evenings. Included in the

prayer meeting besides Berg and Vingren were Ivar Anton Frick Sr., Brother Uldine, and another man (identity undetermined). Brother Uldine gave the prophecy to Vingren. In a meeting with Berg and Vingren a few days later, another prophecy was given that included Berg in the assignment. Special thanks go to Pastor Larry Frick, the grandson of Ivar Anton Frick Sr., for supplying the details of this account.

2. Stanley M. Horton, *The Book of Acts* (Springfield, MO: Gospel Publishing House, 1996), 21.

3. Martyn Lloyd-Jones, *God the Holy Spirit* (Wheaton, IL: Crossway Books, 1997), 238–40.

4. Quoted in ibid., 240.

5. G. Campbell Morgan and Charles H. Spurgeon, *Understanding the Holy Spirit* (Chattanooga, TN: AMG Publishers, 1995), 136.

6. "The Millennium: 100 Events That Changed the World," *Life, The Millennium*, special issue (Fall 1997), 57.

7. William Barclay, *The Acts of the Apostles, The Daily Study Bible* (Philadelphia: Westminster Press, 1976), 12.

8. Horton, *The Book of Acts*, 22.

9. Abridged from Dan Van Veen, ed., *"Do You Know This Man?" American Horizon* (Springfield, MO: Assemblies of God, n.d.), 10–11.

10. Barclay, *The Acts of the Apostles*, 12–13.

11. Morgan and Spurgeon, *Understanding the Holy Spirit*, 134–35.

12. Ibid., 135.

13. *Spirit-Filled Life Bible*, Jack W. Hayford, gen. ed. (Nashville: Thomas Nelson, 1991), 1622.

14. Morgan and Spurgeon, *Understanding the Holy Spirit*, 293.

Chapter 10
The Impact: Worldwide Outreach

1. Frank Damazio, in *Seasons of Revival* (Portland, OR: BT Publishing, 1996), reports that an estimated twenty-eight thousand are coming to Christ in China daily, twenty thousand in Africa, and thirty-five thousand in Latin America: cited in *Ministry Advantage* 7, no. 2 (March/April 1997), 3, a journal of Fuller Theological Seminary.

2. Bob Houlihan was the Assemblies of God field director for the Pacific Rim countries from 1987 to 1997. Similar salvation percentages were quoted in *Ministry Advantage* 7, no. 2 (March/April 1997).

3. Damazio, *Seasons of Revival*, 50–52.

4. Neil Anderson, "Signs of a Worldwide Great Awakening," *Ministry Advantage* 7, no. 2 (March/April 1997), 2.

5. Ibid., 1.

6. "The Millennium: 100 Events That Changed the World," *Life, The Millennium*, special issue (Fall 1997).

7. Harvey Cox, *Fire from Heaven* (Reading, MA: Addison-Wesley, 1994), 167–168.

8. Ibid., 168.

9. Pedro C. Moreno, "The Americas: Pentecostals Redefine Religion in Latin America," *Wall Street Journal*, 29 August 1997, A11.

10. Ibid.

11. H. B. London, "The Pastor's Weekly Briefing," *Focus on the Family Radio Broadcast*: The Word From Washington: "Sexual Predator," Gary L. Bauer, 31 October 1997.

12. H. B. London, *Pastor to Pastor*, Fact Sheet: The Persecuted Church (Focus on the Family, Fall 1997).

13. Ibid.

14. Ibid. Report taken from Religious Liberty Commission of World Evangelical Fellowship.

15. Ibid.

16. H. B. London, "The Pastor's Weekly Briefing," *Focus on the Family Radio Broadcast*: "Global Christian Persecution," Guests: Michael Horowitz, Gary Bauer, Chuck Colson, Rep. Frank Wolf, 16 September 1996.

17. Please do not misunderstand me on this point. We must do all that we can to stop religious persecution. We need to pray for our brothers and sisters throughout the world. We need to write letters to our representatives in Congress and to other government officials. We need to do anything that is legally permissible to prevent these and other countries from persecuting people of faith.

18. Edythe Draper, *Draper's Book of Quotations for the Christian World* (Wheaton, IL: Tyndale, 1992), 659.

19. Ibid., 657.

20. Dr. James Dobson's Bulletin, *Focus on the Family*, November 1997.

21. Ibid.

22. Draper, *Draper's Book of Quotations*, 536.

23. Ibid.

24. From Hal Donaldson and Kenneth M. Dobson, Huldah Buntain, *Woman of Courage* (Sacramento: Onward Books, 1995), 154–56.